O9-BHK-486

HOW COULD YOU REACH OUT AND TOUCH A CHILD LIKE:

Brian, *a nine-year-old who had eaten nothing but saltines and chocolate milk since he was a baby, who flapped his arms and squawked like a bird* . . . Alice, *who spent her whole day drawing different colored breasts* . . . Rufus, *who dressed like a miniature middle-aged businessman, and acted like a violent infant* . . . Jenny, *who walked in a permanent crouch because she was convinced she was a dog* . . .

One of the most moving, powerful, and profoundly enlightening books, not only about disturbed children but all children, ever written.

A CIRCLE OF CHILDREN

"A remarkable book"— *Publishers Weekly* . . .
"Fiercely honest and intense"
　　　　　　　　—*Kirkus Reviews* . . .
"The children in this book altered the author's life, and they will affect yours"— *Psychology Today*

SIGNET Books You'll Want to Read

A Circle of Children

by

Mary MacCracken

A SIGNET BOOK

NEW AMERICAN LIBRARY

TIMES MIRROR

SIGNET TRADEMARK REG. U.S. PAT. OFF. AND FOREIGN COUNTRIES
REGISTERED TRADEMARK—MARCA REGISTRADA
HECHO EN CHICAGO, U.S.A.

SIGNET, SIGNET CLASSICS, MENTOR, PLUME, MERIDIAN AND NAL
BOOKS *are published by The New American Library, Inc.,
1633 Broadway, New York, New York 10019*

FIRST SIGNET PRINTING, MARCH, 1975

12   13   14   15   16   17   18   19   20

PRINTED IN THE UNITED STATES OF AMERICA

101125

For my mother and first teacher:
Florence Ferguson Burnham

He drew a circle that shut me out—
Heretic, rebel, a thing to flout.
But Love and I had the wit to win:
We drew a circle that took him in!

—Edwin Markham

Chapter ONE

I encountered the school without warning, sandwiching the appointment between one at the Y and another at the Cerebral Palsy Clinic, where I had been many times before. It was to be a routine visit; my tennis racket was packed in the back seat of the car in case we finished early enough for a set before our children arrived home from school.

And now, nothing can erase that room, that school. In the slide file of my mind it has a perfect print: each line and shadow as clear now as it was on that first morning. Sunlight slanted across the blue-painted floor surrounding the woman at the piano dressed in a flowered blouse, rose and green, and a green cotton skirt. Small chairs were placed in a semicircle around the piano, and in them sat perhaps twenty children and six or seven adults. The adults, particularly the man, had their knees bunched up to their chins, and yet they seemed comfortable, smiling, calling back and forth across the room to each other.

But there was something strange about the children. It was not their bodies; no one was deformed. In fact, most were beautifully made. There was a translucent quality in their faces, but there was also something more, or perhaps less: a stillness in their expression. These children did not call to each other or playfully poke or tease; instead they sat silently, turned inward.

7

Suddenly the room became filled with noise and motion. Chairs were shoved to the edge of the room while the Director thumped loudly on the piano. The children galloped in pairs around and around until suddenly one tiny girl broke away and flung herself to the floor, screaming high-pitched, indecipherable screams. Her small legs, clad in red tights, were rigid, spread-eagled against the blue floor. She pulled her plaid skirt over her head and beneath it screamed:

"Vacuum cleaner. Look! Aaaaahhh. Aaaahhhh. Get it! Oooohhh. Aaaaahhhh. Get it! Here it comes! Aaaa. Aaaa." She sat up, pointing toward the door. Her terror was real: I felt it inside me, and I turned toward the door, expecting to see a monster vacuum cleaner rolling in, motor running, upright, unstoppable, sucking us all into its giant bag.

But there was nothing, and gradually the terror in the room dissolved. The piano quieted and moved to the smoother rhythm of a waltz, and the children changed from galloping to a skating motion, pushing their feet across the blue floor. No one had stopped to look at the small girl in the middle of the floor or for the vacuum cleaner: they skated on, stepping over her arm or leg if they were jostled and pushed too close to her.

Only her teacher knelt beside her, talking softly, touching her shoulder, her hair. Then gathering her up, she held the child against her own body until the terror dissolved, was gone. As surely as I had seen the vacuum cleaner, I felt the loving that had displaced the terror. In that instant, that clear, bright second, with no warning, I knew that I would one day work in this school. I felt I had been here before, some other time or else some other place; it was familiar. I was at home.

They stayed like that, the child standing, the

woman kneeling with her arms about the child for perhaps a minute more; then the little girl's enormous eyes left the door and she put her hand against the teacher's head. They rose then and, hand in hand, rejoined the circle of skaters.

The woman beside me touched my arm. "My God, Mary, I can't take much more of this. Let's get out of here."

I turned to look at her, my friend Ellen, here with me on the assignment from the Junior League to investigate the school for seriously emotionally disturbed children, to visit and see if it would have good placement jobs for our volunteers; and she seemed suddenly far away. I had known her since I was a child, I had been with her when she bought the tweed skirt and blue cashmere sweater that she was wearing; and yet when she spoke to me it was as if her words were coming from a distant country. How could we leave? It seemed to me that we were on the brink of an enormous secret.

Then as my thoughts returned to her, I saw that she had been moved, but not to wonder. Revulsion showed in her face, and I did not know how to tell her about the excitement that I felt.

I followed her away from the room, out onto the porch of the big old white-frame building that housed the school. She said again:

"Mary, this place is terrible. They're crazy. Those children are crazy. Mad. Just little kids and they're completely gone. No one in the League could work here. Think what it would be like to go home to your children after this. Come on, let's go. We'll have lunch and then we'll go to the C. P. Clinic and still have time to get in some tennis before the kids get home."

Crazy. Were they? And what does "crazy" mean?

Did she think perhaps that it was catching—that we might take it home to our children, like measles or a bad cold? What was it? What caused it?

"You go," I said. "I'll just be a few minutes, talk to the Director, get some pamphlets and a little information, and then I'll meet you for lunch, okay?"

Ellen looked at me curiously. "You're going back in there? What for? There's no point." Then perhaps recognizing some stubbornness in me reminiscent of our childhood, she sighed. "Oh all right. You're a good, responsible placement chairman. Where do you want to eat?"

Ah, good. She was going. "Doesn't matter. Anywhere. You choose."

"Well, I did want to pick up a wedding present for Betsy at Jensen's. Suppose I do that—then I'll meet you at Lord and Taylor's and we can eat there."

"Great," I said. "I'll see you in an hour."

I stood on the steps of the school watching Ellen pull out of the driveway, excited, but knowing that there was still time to change my mind. Instead of going back inside, I, too, could leave. I could get into my car, raise the white convertible top, and drive my way back to my safe, suburban life. I could surprise Ellen at Jensen's, and while she shopped I could linger, drinking in the lovely things, touching a silver bowl, running my finger along the edge of a crystal vase when the salesman turned away, comfortable in a familiar world.

And what if I went back inside? What then? What kind of world lay there, just a few feet away? If I opened the door what would I find—what would I learn?

I lingered a moment more on the steps—then I turned and went back inside the school.

The Director's office was in the basement, past the lunchroom. There was a musty smell; and though the walls had been painted yellow to compensate for the lack of windows, there was a distinct greenish cast to both the walls and the air. I stood in the doorway of the office; the Director, Mrs. Fleming, was on the phone and I waited hesitantly in the doorway until she finished.

The rest of the memory is blurred. I know I asked many questions and she replied with words like "emotionally disturbed," "schizophrenic," "autistic," which rolled across my ears as sounds rather than words, almost meaningless to me then. She mentioned the school's tremendous financial needs, the ratio of four children to one teacher, the newness of the field, the lack of agreement as to causes: some experts citing heredity, others environment, still others, biochemical causes. She spoke of the waiting list of children they could not accommodate and her dream of a new building, a larger school.

"The children?" I asked. "Can you tell me a little more about the children?"

"Well, as you can see," she said, "they are physically healthy, attractive children. Their intelligence is average or above average, but they're ill, and this illness causes them to function far below their age level, to live inside themselves and shut out the world. They are not sure who they are. They have great difficulty with language, with relationships, with other people; their behavior is often bizarre, puzzling."

I stayed well over an hour, fascinated, intrigued, forgetting the time until I heard the children gathering in the lunchroom.

But excitement bubbled inside me, could not be put down. I wanted to teach there. Absurd? Perhaps. But I wanted it, had to do it, knew that I could. Unsure of many things, I was sure of this. One last question: What qualifications did her teachers need?

The Director smiled. "Certification in special education—preferably a master's degree in teaching the emotionally disturbed—a listening heart and a strong back."

I thanked her. My own heart was very quiet. I hadn't even finished Wellesley, having left at the end of my sophomore year to marry Larry.

Chapter *TWO*

But all summer long the children of the school walked through my dreams, and in September I went back to the school to ask if I could work there as a volunteer teacher's aide two days a week. The morning was warm and the windows of the school were open, and I heard again the piano as I climbed the wide wooden steps.

More strongly than ever the *déjà-vu* feeling returns; perhaps not this same school, but somewhere, sometime, I worked in a school such as this. There is a remembered knowledge that is certain without being specific.

I find the Director in her office.

"Good morning," she says. "Can I help you?"

"I'm Mary MacCracken," I remind her. "I was here last June. I . . . uh. Well, what I wondered was . . . do you think it would be possible for me to work as a volunteer with one of your teachers?"

"Oh, yes, I remember now. You were here with the other woman from the Junior League. Yes. Well now, let's see. Yes . . . I think we'll put you as a teacher's aide with Helga. We're delighted to have you, Mrs. . . . er—uh . . ."

"Mary," I say. "My name is Mary."

"Yes, of course. Mary. Go right on up to Helga's room. As I say, we're delighted to have you."

I climbed the empty stairs slowly. There was no one in the room at the top of the stairs. As I stood in the hall indecisively a boy of perhaps nine or ten raced by me, his turtleneck shirt pulled completely over his head, screaming, "Jesus Christ, gonna go to Camp Lookout! God save us all!" He thundered down the stairs, and I wondered how he was able to judge their height and depth with his eyes covered.

A man came out of one of the rooms along the hall, smiled at me, and called softly to the boy: "Hey, Tom, it's okay. Camp's over, you're in school," and he walked slowly down the stairs toward the boy, who was now hesitating on the bottom step.

I continued walking along the long upstairs hall, looking in classrooms, searching for Helga's room. They were all empty except for one classroom. A small girl watched in fascination an empty turntable revolve. A gray-eyed boy sat beside her, smiling and rocking back and forth, back and forth, until a young woman rose from the table where she was mixing paints and touched him, blocked the rocking with her hand, and he followed her back to the paint table.

A kaleidoscope of impressions was whirling through my head. Was this teacher Helga? And would she, too, be "delighted" to have me? As it turned out, she was not.

I found her finally in the bathroom with her class of four children. She was bent over the toilet bowl with a rubber plunger.

"God damn fucking stopped-up toilet. How can you toilet-train a child when the stupid toilet doesn't even flush? Who are you?"

"Mary," I answer. "The Director sent me to be your new volunteer teacher's aide."

Helga wields the rubber plunger even harder now—brown-gray hair flying straight out from her head, glasses slipping to the end of her nose. She must be fifty, arms strong and muscular, moving up and down, everything about her alive, filled with vitality. She is wearing a cotton housedress, and under it I can see wide shoulders, full breasts, narrower waist and hips—her legs strong and bare above worn, wet sneakers.

"For Christ sake," she says in a strong German accent. "How many times do I have to tell her I don't want any shitty volunteers? I have enough to do with the children. Go on now. Go tell her to assign you to somebody else."

But I do not want to go. Intuitively I recognize in Helga the essence of the master teacher. I know that she is the one I want to watch; hers are the techniques I want to learn. In this school I do not feel humble or frightened or inadequate, as I often do with Larry. I am at home here and I merely smile at Helga and follow her back to her classroom, watching her quietly. I had never heard a woman swear like that before. The women I had known most intimately were lovely, quiet women—clean and soft, smelling faintly sweet, dressed always in good taste. I survey Helga in her cotton housedress and worn sneakers, and for the first time I wonder what "good taste" means.

Sunlight lies across the green linoleum floor. The walls are covered with children's primitive finger painting; a large rocking chair is in front of the window, a low table with chairs in the middle of the room, a sandbox on the far side.

One of the boys stands in the sunlight watching the specks of dust move in the golden air currents. He is very small, perhaps five or six, with a small, square face and large gray eyes, black at the center.

Helga speaks to him. "Take off your sweater, Chris. Hang it up on the hook."

Still he stands without moving, arms slack; only his eyes follow the golden specks of dust. I do not move to help, only watch as I sit on a corner of the sandbox, filling a muffin tin with sand and turning my muffins on a wooden board. Red-haired Jimmy sticks a crayon in each one and then pushes them back to the center of the sandpile.

Helga ignores Chris, giving him a chance to act on his own volition. She notices me and is obviously annoyed that I am still there. She no longer even addresses me directly but instead mutters toward the window concerning me.

"God in heaven. Give me patience. It is not enough that I must teach these children all day with no equipment, only leftover material and promises. Now they send me volunteers. Over and over I have told them I do not want the shitty volunteers. Volunteers to do for the children what they should do for themselves. Do they listen? No. Jesus, deliver me from these volunteers. They should take their shitty good works somewhere else."

The last is delivered pointedly in my direction and I bend my head in concentration on my muffins.

One last remark from Helga: "Ah—well. It does not usually take us too long to get rid of them, does it?"

Helga chooses now to ignore me. All morning she never looks again in my direction. Instead, she turns once again to Chris. Her voice lifts, half a command, half a seduction: "Come now—get off that sweater and we'll have a bit of a rock before the day begins."

Chris slides his eyes from the dust specks toward Helga, not moving, only looking.

She settles herself in the rocking chair and sets it in motion. "Come along now," she calls, "get along."

And, unbelievably, the slack, motionless figure becomes a boy. Awkwardly he takes off his sweater and hangs it on a hook beneath his name, CHRIS, and then crosses the room and climbs into the wide lap of Helga. And with her legs spread wide and her foot tapping she sings to him:

"Camptown races is my song—do dah, do dah. Camptown races all day long, all the do dah day." And if the words are wrong, it does not bother Helga or Chris.

I watch them and then, noticing an empty coffee can lying beside the sandbox, I go next door to the bathroom and fill it with water.

"Not this one," I say to myself as the water runs into the can. "You will not be rid of this volunteer so easily, Helga." And I smile at her as I carry the water back to the sandbox.

So began our relationship, Helga's and mine, and my education. I learned more from this strong, loving woman than from any psychology or education course I have ever taken; more than from any book, no matter how distinguished the author. I watched her, remembering, imitating, gradually doing. She breathed life back into the children. Often I watched her gather a child in her arms—one who had gone off to a corner, retreating from the world, perhaps beginning to masturbate to start the dreams, to bring the fantasy world closer. Helga would gather him up, blow on his neck, murmur some foolish joke into his ear, take his hand, start the record player, and then dance with him around the room. Her favorite dance was the polka, and as she skipped and stomped in her sneakers, gray hair flying, half carrying her small partner with her, she would sing, "There's a garden, what a garden, only happy faces bloom there, and there's never any gloom there . . ." And gradually the child would return, the faraway look would go out of his eyes, and he would seem once more to be alive, to be back in this world.

There was about Helga such a strong sense of living, of vitality, that as she came into bodily contact with a child—rocking him, holding him from attacking himself or others, kissing him, pushing him—her vitality, her excitement, her desire of life were almost visibly transferred to the child. She could not have told me any of this herself; she was totally absorbed in her work, in her children—so much so that even at the end of the same day, if someone had asked her to describe what methods or techniques she had used to solve a problem, she would not have been able to relate what she had done. She would not even have tolerated the words "methods" and "techniques"; she was the totally natural therapeutic teacher. I was privileged to be able to watch her, and I knew it. A dozen times a day I would find myself silently saying, "Yes, yes," as I watched her with the children. It was a feeling of silent applause and I knew I must pay attention to it.

She had that rare quality of being alive, involved in, excited by, her world. Whether this is learned or an inherited talent I am not sure, but it was one of her most valuable tools in reaching these children: the electricity that was vibrant in her reached across and touched the child, often before words could.

Helga's husband Karl worked at a clerical job; their only son was grown, living in the West. They lived in a small upstairs apartment in a two-family house, saving money all year in order to travel. Each winter during Christmas vacation they went to Puerto Rico; in the summer they rode bicycles across Europe. Looking at Helga, I would think of my own friends, my own life, our large homes, all our possessions—and yet Helga had achieved a freedom, a sense of joy, that was absent in my own life.

It was not that she always had an admirable response or even a proper one. She did not. She was no saint. But the thing was, she did respond! She was alive, she was human, she cared, and she showed us that she did. There were no pretenses to Helga. What she felt, she communicated, and because there was no veneer it came through straight and clear.

If a child, as he gradually learned or rediscovered words, came to Helga saying, "Kite," Helga would listen, repeat, "You like the kite. Ah—get it then. Get the kite. Let's see it now, this red kite."

And now Jimmy, excited by the sight and feel of the kite, tugs Helga's arm: "Kite. Fly kite. Fly kite."

Helga sits back on her heels from where she has been kneeling beside the boy and says, "Ah, fly the kite. So you think we should fly the kite, leave our papers and crayons, and go fly the kite. Is that what you think?"

Jimmy, ordinarily listless, pale as milk beneath his red hair, hops up and down with excitement. "Fly kite, Helga. Go fly kite."

Helga grins, satisfied with her work, with the extra words she has managed to extract from Jimmy, and says, "All right, you monkey—we'll leave the work and go fly the kite."

And soon all of us—the four children, myself, and Helga—have on our jackets and are trudging out to the field beyond the school, Jimmy carrying the kite. Then they run, the small red-haired boy and Helga in her sneakers. They run holding the string of the kite together, getting it started—until suddenly the kite lifts and sails up high, like hope itself, flashing, tipping against the sky, and we cheer and clap our hands.

I cannot remember now how many weeks it was before Helga spoke to me. I remember that I felt no resentment because of her silence. It seemed to me a logical thing: she was trying to do something important, and volunteers got in her way; it was natural that she be impatient with me. At the same time I had no intention of leaving.

There were other teachers in the school who were good. I watched them at Circle and at the playground and at lunch, but none of them rang the bell for me the way Helga did. Her children grew faster than any others, became independent sooner—or so it seemed to me. I knew I could learn more from her than from anyone else. Whether she liked me or not was not essential. I was not lonely. I did not need her friendship; I needed her example.

For instance, I watched her teach Sarah to walk. Sarah did not walk at all when she first came to school. She was five, with pale yellow hair and the fine, silky skin of a baby. She was a week late starting school because she had been ill, so I was there when she came that first day. Her mother carried her up the stairs to Helga's room, spread a blanket, and laid her on the floor. There Sarah curled up on her side, her thumb in her mouth. Helga said nothing; but after the mother had left, Helga slipped the blanket from beneath Sarah, folded it, and put it in the back of a closed cupboard. The little girl whimpered and cried, the other children circling around her as I have seen a flock of sea gulls do when one of the birds is injured. The morning was ruined, the children upset and fretful; no work could be done with Sarah mewling, crying, there on the floor. Another teacher might have let her keep the blanket that first day while she adjusted to the school. Not Helga. She would set no such precedent in her classroom—a five-year-old child was not treated like an infant, left lying in a blanket.

Finally Sarah moved. Painfully, slowly, she crawled across the floor, stopping every few minutes to rest, then continuing her slow, tortuous journey as we watched, holding our breath. She made her way directly to the cabinet where Helga had put her blanket, and scratched with her tiny hands at the door. Helga picked her up then and carried her to the rocking chair, talking to her, mixing German words with English:

"Come now—come now, little one. It is all right. Everything will be all right. I know you now; you cannot fool Helga. You are smart and you can move. You try to fool us, *ja?* Lying there, sucking on your thumb. But you are smart, *ja?* You know just where I hid that blanket, and when you want it enough and I do not bring it to you, then you yourself go to get it. *Ja, ja,* my little one, my pretty golden one, we will teach you to talk and to walk."

Helga rocked her then and sang to her. Each morning after that, Helga greeted Sarah at the front door and carried her up the stairs herself. She did not wish to explain to Sarah's mother what had happened to the blanket—that it now lay discarded beneath a box of old records in the recesses of the cabinet. Before long, it would disappear altogether. Dealing with parents or the public was not one of Helga's strong points; she left that to the Director.

Sarah crawled more and more on the green linoleum in Helga's room, gradually strengthening arms, legs, curiosity, as she explored the room. A small rag doll was her favorite toy. She would find it and play with it long hours at a time. One morning, before Sarah arrived, Helga moved the doll from the floor to the top of one of the low cabinets. Another frustrating, miserable day for all of us—worse than the first because now Sarah had a temper. She not only whimpered and whined; she screamed and kicked her heels against the floor in rage—but two days later she stood for the first time, pulling herself up until she could reach the top of the cabinet, reach her doll. And when she had it safe in one hand, balancing herself with the other to stay upright, she laughed out loud in triumph. Helga let her have her triumph, shaking her head, saying, "Ah, you, Sarah, such a girl. You are too smart for me. Too smart for old Helga. You find that doll no matter where I put it."

From crawling to walking to climbing that long flight of stairs to Helga's room. At first Helga stayed where she could cushion the fall if it occurred. Then, as confidence grew, she moved on ahead so that Sarah could see her there, have incentive to move ahead—not begging or pleading with the child, simply waiting, expecting her to be able to do it. And she did. Even then Helga's praise was short— one word: "Good!"—brief, clipped: "Hang up your coat now. We're late for Circle."

Helga, wise, strong, letting Sarah savor the pride in her own accomplishment, not setting up a new dependency. Even the morning, many months later, when Sarah came up the whole flight, breaking away from her mother at the door, walking fast, climbing without holding on, up the stairs, up to Helga—even then her kiss on Sarah's neck was brief, and she said only, "You've a lot of energy today, girl. Come and help me." And they went together to do battle against the toilet.

Helga and I had one thing in common, and it was one of the things that made me sure that I must work under her, learn from her, rather than from another teacher. Helga and I had the same basic language. Even though our native tongues were different—she born in Germany, I in America—we both had a body language and communicated best through it, trusting it more than words. It was less tricky, more complete. It is more than merely touch: people touch each day and communicate nothing. Body language is the first language—the way the

mother speaks to the child long before he can understand her words. As she holds him, bathes him, feeds
him, she is telling him of love or anger or irritation.
So, too, Helga spoke to her seriously emotionally disturbed children, many of whom had rejected verbal
communication, and they listened to this body language. Most of her touching was light and firm and
quick. She used it to communicate affection, support,
pride in the child; usually she touched the back,
shoulders, arm, or head; she used it alone or with a
few simple words. She also used another kind of
touching. It was really more holding. It said in ef-
fect, "I am here. We will survive." She reacted this
way during violence, when a child tried to kick her
or bite himself—holding him, restraining him from
the destructive act and at the same time comforting
him with the solidness of her body. When violence
explodes inside a child, all things seem unreal, and
the solid strength and warmth of another human
being who is not driven away or shattered by it
makes the terror more controllable.

Never, however, did she use this body language to
express her own anger or irritation. Striking a child
may cause him to become fearful of your touch, and
this is too valuable a tool to lose, too high a price to
pay for momentary frustration. Instead, Helga
swore. She cursed as I had never heard a woman do
before, and it seemed to harm the children not at
all.

If I do not remember when she first addressed me
directly, I do remember when she first called me by
name.

It was in the spring of that first year, more like
summer really although the official date had not arrived. Yellow daffodils had already flooded the hills
and fields where we had sailed our kite. Nick, our

one male teacher, had put up swings under two of the apple trees, and whenever we could we took the children there in the late morning to play and relax before lunch.

I was pushing Chris on a swing—pushing him from in front instead of from behind so that I could see his face while I played with him. A small game had developed between us: he would straighten and stiffen his legs as the swing approached me, and then laugh out loud as his feet hit my hands and I pushed against them, sending him arcing gently back. Helga had taken the other three children to play some sort of game with Nick's group. Since Chris was not very good at games, always running, hitting, biting, Helga had stated, "It is a good day for a swing for Chris," and I had known I was to do this. I loved being with Chris anyway—his very stubbornness fascinated me. Bright as a button, he refused to speak a word; perfectly toilet-trained for months now, he would deliberately pee on the Director's foot when she brought visitors to our room for "public relations." She handled it well, though, not even blanching as the brown leather of her shoe turned slowly darker and a puddle formed around it as Chris stood still, looking out the window, smiling, with her hand stroking his head.

In any event, I was totally absorbed in my game with Chris and, thinking we were alone, had even started hamming it up a little as I had with my own children, making funny faces, pretending to be knocked backward when his feet hit my hands. I thought he was beginning to say something: was it "More"—"Mo, mo"? I had not heard footsteps, and was startled when I felt a hand on my arm. I turned quickly. Unexpectedly, Helga was standing beside me.

"Mary," she said, calling me by name for the first

time, "these are for you." She stretched out her hand toward me and it was full of small wild strawberries. We ate them there together, standing in the sun, sharing the sharp, sweet taste, the grittiness. Since then I have been given many other gifts and some honors, but none has meant more to me than this. Helga had acknowledged me; I was sure then that I could teach.

Chapter *THREE*

I worked even harder the remainder of that year with Helga. I canceled my Tuesday bridge and my Thursday afternoon tennis foursome and went three days a week to school rather than two.

From the time Elizabeth and Rick had entered school I had always worked as a volunteer, either at the hospital on the library cart or in the county shelter for adolescents. There was strong tradition in our family for community volunteer and board work, and I had always enjoyed it. But the school was different. I had worked at the hospital and the shelter because it had seemed part of a responsible way of living. I worked now at the school because I loved it and couldn't stay away.

If I had studied Helga carefully before, I watched her even more closely those last weeks, for she told me suddenly, one day as we walked with the children, that she would not be back the following year.

"Why?" I asked. It seemed impossible to me. I could not imagine Helga without the children or the children without Helga.

"They want me to go back to school," she said. "An old woman like me. What would they teach me? Ha! What do I need with their fancy courses, their methods-teaching, visual aids, curriculum-planning? They say I will not get my proper salary unless I go to the college and take courses given by some young pup, because our school is about to become approved by the state and I will need the courses for certification. Ach, it is a waste. They can take their shitty courses.

"I know what I am saying. Nick took me to visit the college. The professors either say in fancy language what I already know, or they speak foolishness that is best never heard."

"Where will you go? What will the children do without you?" I asked.

Helga laughed out loud and put her arm around my shoulders, and I could feel the resiliency of her strong, still-lithe body.

"There are plenty of sick children in the world. Come with me on Saturday and I will show you. As for these, my children here, they will be all right. They are almost ready to go now—and if not, she will hire another to teach them."

I could not tell whether it was bitterness I heard in Helga's voice or only disappointment.

On Saturday, Helga picked me up in her ancient coupe and drove me over to her new school; she had met its young director many years before. She led me to the central resource room filled with shelves lined with paper, paints, clay, doll families, puzzles, books, workbooks, textbooks, pencils, blocks, on and on—and outside in the shed beside the building, bicycles, scooters—contrasting to our own meager supplies.

Helga spread her hands. "We are rich!" she said. "Come, come." Down a long hall, then she threw open a door marked GIRLS: there in white-tiled glory were five sinks and seven toilets, and Helga flushed each one with satisfaction.

On Memorial Day weekend Helga went bicycling through northern New England with her husband. She was anxious to be gone, and I knew those last weeks of school were very difficult for her. She might say she didn't mind leaving, but I saw her eyes fill with tears more than once, and her cursing had increased. She decided to add a day and a half to her weekend and asked if I would take charge of her class during that time.

I was pleased to be asked, of course—I was proud that Helga felt that I could teach alone. I knew she cared too much for her children to leave them with anyone she thought incompetent. It was not until much later that I realized that Helga was now consciously teaching me, preparing me, making me grow, just as she did the children. Helga had never taken an education or psychology course, but she was a born teacher, and she knew instinctively when it was time for me to take on more responsibility.

Now, too, I read, researched, balancing what I was reading against Helga's teaching. Helga had not thought much of education courses, and yet I was greedy for every morsel of information I could find on childhood schizophrenia, autism, the emotionally disturbed. I soon exhausted our local libraries and moved on to the libraries of New York, and bought my own books. Still, amazingly little had been written about these illnesses in children, and many of the authorities disagreed with one another on the cause and range, on diagnosis and prognosis. I wished Helga would write her own book. The others were confusing, contradictory—and yet valuable. So I kept on reading—textbooks, case histories, personal experiences—agreeing, disagreeing, gradually evolving my own beliefs, though these, too, I knew would shift and change as more research was done and my own experience grew.

The term "seriously emotionally disturbed child" covers a wide range, including both the withdrawn, autistic child and the hyperactive, violently acting-out child. Many of the children in our school were diagnosed as being autistic, but the Director preferred the broader term "seriously emotionally disturbed."

Although there were differing views, gradually a pattern appeared as I read. Various authorities differed on cause and treatment, but most writers and educators seemed to agree on the prime characteristics of the emotionally disturbed child.

First of all, he has a lack of awareness of his own identity. His concept of his own body image is very small. He seldom speaks properly; sometimes he may not speak at all. Certainly this was true at our school; over two thirds of the children had severe language problems.

The seriously emotionally disturbed child resists change, often becomes preoccupied with a particular object, and is filled with excessive anxiety. His emotional relationships with family, peers, and teachers are severely impaired. He does not care; he is turned in upon himself. Although he may appear to be retarded because of these things, still he may often have flashes of brilliance in contrast to the even performance of the retarded child.

The books said this and I believed it: still, it was a conglomerate, whereas to me each child was unique, an individual.

The more I read, the more certain I became of one fact: the screening and certifying of teachers of emotionally disturbed children should not depend solely upon graduation and completion of required courses; the screening should be different for this field. The Helgas of this world must not be lost. The art of communication is just that—an art—and there must be a talent before the craftsmanship can be developed, or you will have only technicians, not gifted teachers. You can instill a hundred techniques in a teacher, have her memorize thousands of technical terms; but if she cannot make contact with the children they are useless.

We said good-bye on the last day of school, Helga and I. We stood on the paint-stained green linoleum of her classroom and I knew I would never see her just so again. I tried to memorize her—the short, thick, straight, graying hair; the horn-rimmed glasses slipping ever closer to the end of her nose as she bent her head nearer, closer, to get a better look; the strong legs above the sneakers. Not young or fashionable or beautiful—merely ageless and phenomenal, like the mountains I had seen in Canada. She had charted a new course, opened a new door, turned a new leaf; there were no right words, only clichés; but Helga had done it for me—and I loved her.

I had wanted to give her a present but I could not think of the right one, and so I went to her now and put my arms around her and out loud could only say, "Thank you, Helga." But I hope my body language spoke to her.

She held me, too, and we stood like this. Then she moved back a little and took my chin and held it in her hand, smiled, and said, "You will be a good teacher, Mary. Yes. Just watch out for the shitty volunteers."

Chapter *FOUR*

In the fall I went back to work at the school again, but it was very different. Not only had Helga left, but most of the staff left with her, having been lured to higher-paying positions. The Director remained, strong, resolute, and for the first time I could imagine her founding the school. She hired a new staff—new psychologists, teachers, psychiatrist, speech therapist.

Besides a new staff, there was also a new location. One of the board members had been instrumental in persuading a church in a nearby town to let the school use its building during the week. It was new and clean and pleasant. There were only two drawbacks: there was no kitchen—all the lunches had to be brought in—and nothing could be left in the classrooms over the weekends; they had to be cleared for Sunday school. Each Friday everything had to be taken down, rolled up, packed away, carried down a long hall to be stored in a back room; then early on Monday mornings the process was reversed.

I was assigned to work with Renée when I went back, and for the first time I learned what bad teaching was. She was young and pretty with teased blond hair; but instead of the happy, confident security I had come to take for granted as the school's atmosphere, there was a tight, brittle tension in Renée's room behind what she called "permissiveness." I watched her narrow hands clench and her voice rise as she refilled the bathtub of water she kept in the center of the room; time and time again the children dumped it over with shrill laughter.

Her theory of permissiveness, she explained, was one that was used with great success in Canada. She felt that all emotional disturbance stemmed from the same source: the fact that the child had never been accepted by his parents. So before he could grow up, he must be allowed to be a baby and do the things he had wanted to do. Renée brought with her pink tin playhouse equipment—stove, refrigerator, sink. I was not quite sure how these fitted into her theory, but I know that my major contribution to her class that fall was the lugging of stove, refrigerator, sink, and bathtub back and forth on Fridays and Mondays.

I was not happy working in that room. All day long the children destroyed things. "They are getting the hate out of their systems," Renée would say; but if they were, they did not seem any happier for it. They whined and cried and lay on the floor, cold and wet with bath water and urine.

Just before Christmas vacation I spoke to the Director, asking to be transferred to another room. I did not feel knowledgeable enough to be critical—it was possible that this was another way to teach, perhaps a valid way, but it was not for me. And by now my own self-knowledge had grown to the point where I did not wish to pretend. At least not here at school.

There was a great deal of snow that Christmas and our town was white and beautiful. The schools, of course, were closed for the holiday and the house was filled with the noises of my own two children and their friends.

Rick was the oldest, a senior in high school—tall,

solidly built, good in both sports and his studies. He was one of those rare children who seemed to have been born happy, well adjusted in his own world, tolerant of others.

Elizabeth was four years younger, and whereas Rick was broad, thick through the shoulders, Elizabeth was slender with black hair, blue eyes; always late, always rushing, eager, stormy, both sensitive and critical—and the most tender and loving of us all. Her Christmas presents expressed her intimate knowledge of us, each gift specific and personal—exactly what each of us had wanted but had not had the time or money or courage to buy.

Larry left early each day for his office in the city, and so I ate a second, long, lazy breakfast with the kids, lingering over the pancakes, a luxury for which there was never time during school. I savored both my coffee and my children, knowing that after breakfast they would be gone into the city for a basketball game or a movie, or else skating at the club with their friends.

Thoughts of the school receded slightly from my mind until one morning just after New Year's Day when the phone rang. It was the President of the Board of Trustees of the school saying that there was a vacancy on the Board and asking if I would be willing to fill it. I did not really want the position. I had served on too many boards already, gone to too many meetings, voted too many times; but this was the school, and the thought crossed my mind that perhaps this was as far as I would get there, my dreams of teaching too impossible. At least this way I could help build a new school, for our present quarters were only temporary. I watched a brown female cardinal in the pine tree just outside the window beside the telephone, and said, "Yes, I would be delighted to serve."

I never did, though.

Before that same day ended, the Director of the school called. She said that Joyce, one of the new teachers, had been in a bad automobile accident; her car had skidded out of control and she had slammed head on into a highway divider. The car was a total loss, Joyce's injuries serious but not permanent. Still, they would take time to heal; she would be in the hospital for six weeks. Could I take her class during that time at substitute's salary?

The thing I had wanted so badly had happened; the job I had hoped for had been offered to me. So this is how it happens, I thought, no heavenly choir like in the movies, just quietly—a voice on the telephone. I, too, spoke quietly, using mundane language.

"I'll speak to my family," I said, "and call you this evening."

Again I was surprised how small a thing it seemed to them. The kids said merely that they thought it was great. They loved to hear stories of the school and had been over to visit a couple of times.

When I told Larry that I had been asked to teach, he barely looked up from the television set. I lingered uncertainly, feeling in some way that I should warn him that this would change me. I was not sure how, but if the days as a volunteer with Helga had influenced me as much as they had, surely a full-time job would do more. But the commercial came on and he watched even that with concentration.

I called the Director then and asked more questions about Joyce's class. Which children were in it? What were they like?

Billy, Chris, Louis, and Brad.

I knew none of them except Chris—the same Chris I had pushed on the swing when I was in Helga's class. I had seen him only once or twice this year because his room was at the opposite end of the building from Renée's. My head spun—so much to find out, but I couldn't do it on the phone; no point in holding the Director. I thanked her and asked when it would be possible to come and talk with her.

"Oh, I'll see you in the morning," she replied.

"Tomorrow morning?" I asked.

"Yes. Vacation ends today, you know. The children will all be back tomorrow. You will start then."

Chapter FIVE

I arrived early that first morning, thinking to talk with the Director, to find out about the children in Joyce's class, to learn their backgrounds, their case histories, the results of their psychological and physical examinations. Even more important was to learn what their routine in school had been, what they were used to, how Joyce handled their problems, the daily lesson plan.

The Director was on the phone when I walked into her office, and I realized that this was my most familiar memory of her, both in this new building and in the old school. As I passed the office I would see her at her desk writing, talking—cigarette and pencil alternating in her right hand, the phone in her left.

She had white hair cut short, pushed back from a small, attractive face, bright brown eyes, and was somewhere between forty and sixty years old. She was cheerful and articulate in her speech; her movements were quick, strong, and spontaneous. She smiled and waved a good morning to me across the phone and cigarette and motioned to me to hang up my coat. I hung my heavy storm coat in the closet in her office, took off my fur-lined gloves and high brown boots, and—in memory of Helga—put on my sneakers. With my sneakers on, I was ready to teach.

The Director's voice continued on the phone: "You're right, it's freezing cold this morning. If he's coughing you're wise to keep him home. Mmmmm. Yes. He did? Last night?"

Another ten minutes passed. I was beginning to get restless. In twenty minutes my class would arrive. I didn't even know their last names.

Finally the phone call ended and the Director smiled at me. "I'm so glad you were able to come, Mary. How about a cup of coffee? First thing I do every morning when I get here is to plug in the pot." From the shelf behind her desk she produced two cups and poured coffee for each of us.

"Could you tell me a little about the children in Joyce's class?" I asked.

"Well, there are four boys . . . oh, excuse me, the phone. Oh, dear, I forgot to make a note that Jeff won't be in; I must remember to tell Dan. Lots of calls on these cold mornings . . ."

And she was gone again. The phone rang four more times. There was a minor crisis when the woman who was scheduled to bring the casserole lunch for the children called to say that she herself was sick and couldn't get out.

"Don't worry. You take care of yourself now. Thanks for calling. Oh—yes. Yes. Certainly. No problem at all. Get well in a hurry now." Cheeriness continued to flow out of the Director's voice over the haze of cigarette smoke.

As soon as she was off the phone she was putting on her coat. "I'm going to have to dash over to the store and then back home for a minute to pick up the hot plate. The woman from the church who was supposed to bring lunch is sick, or so she says, so we'll have to heat up some soup. Tell Zoe to handle the phone till I get back; she'll be in in a minute. Oh, and I'll see you at Circle with your class." She emphasized the last two words and smiled.

"Mrs. Fleming . . ." I said.

"No, no. Call me Doris. Here now—here are the folders on the children ..." She rummaged in a green file cabinet behind her desk. "Let's see now—Chris, you remember him. From Helga's class. Brad, he's a doll. Where's Billy's—ah—here it is. And let's see. Who else is there? Oh, yes, Louis. Mmmmm. Can't find his at the moment. Oh, well, it's not important. These will give you a start."

She left then, leaving me holding the pale manila folders in my hand.

At the front door she turned back. "Don't worry. Everything will be fine."

I had wished for information, not cheery platitudes, and yet I had a small glimpse of the courage of the woman who had somehow not only founded the school but kept it together through many desperate times when money had been nonexistent and her own personal life rocked with the tragedy of her husband's death. Perhaps she had found it necessary to ignore certain needs in order to be able to cope with bigger problems—perhaps cheeriness was the mask she wore.

Nonetheless, I shivered in my red jumper as I followed her out the door, calling, "Which is my room. Which door?"

"Oh, my. I forgot that, didn't I? Well, you can't remember everything. Especially on these cold mornings. The last one in the back is Joyce's. Yours, I mean."

I went back inside with a sinking heart. How could I have been so presumptuous as to think I could handle all this? It was one thing under Helga's direction. But alone? I knew the Director scarcely at all. Helga had always referred to her by title or as "they," which I had taken to signify authority. Now I wondered. She had left without introducing me to the children, without giving me any idea of the day's routine.

Well, I decided, I would go down to the classroom and look at the folders. Perhaps I could at least learn how to recognize Brad from Louis.

The room was L-shaped, painted green. There were two high windows on the north wall so that the room was light enough, but cold and wintry. There was a large wooden jungle gym in one corner, a small white bookcase which held a few Golden books, and two Maxwell House coffee cans with wooden beads, strings, pegs, and missing puzzle pieces. There were three wooden puzzles and a peg board. Beside the bookcase was a small wooden chest that held some blocks, a doll with a missing head, a small, soiled blanket, and half a dozen clean diapers. There was also a jumping-jack rocking horse and a small pink table with chairs. A complete inventory. It had taken me less than three minutes to make it. Helga's materials were sparse, but they were four times this. I looked again at the chest and book-shelves—could I teach four children with just these odds and ends?

There were coat hooks along one wall, though, and these at least looked familiar—until I saw that there were more than a dozen and they were labeled with names like Susan and Diane. Obviously names from the Sunday school class. Where did Joyce's boys hang their coats? On nameless hooks or under some-one else's name?

Slam! The door of the room slammed shut so hard the glass in the window of the door rattled. A tall, dark man stood inside the door leaning against it, holding a small boy by the arm. It was Chris; I could not mistake those gray eyes—but if he recognized me he gave no sign of it.

"I'm Chris's father," the man said. "Will you tell his teacher he's here?"

Chris twisted his body away from his father, trying to loosen his arm, pulling at the doorknob, trying to get the door open, to get out.

And I think, What is this? I have known this child before—he was always difficult, disruptive, but he never fought school before. What is this now?

Out loud I say, "Joyce isn't in today. I'm Mary MacCracken, the substitute teacher."

His eyes travel over me. "Well ... good luck," he says. Then: "Look, could you just hold the door while I get out, then I can hold it closed from the other side till you can slip the bolt?"

For the first time I see a brass sliding bolt near the top of the door, and something inside of me is outraged. I may be new, I may be inexperienced, but I do not need to lock my children in a room to keep them there.

I smile at the man, still not knowing his last name, and say, "That's all right. You just go on ahead. Thank you for bringing Chris." And I see my brave, foolish words reflected in his gray eyes that are much like Chris's.

I knelt on the floor beside Chris and put my arm around his waist. The father, in one swift movement, was out the door, holding it closed from the outside, peering in through the window.

Chris gave a tremendous lurch, trying to reach freedom, but my hand fastened on his belt and I held on, even as I toppled over and spread flat against the floor.

Damn that window, I thought, knowing that the father was watching—but I held on tight. It was important, what we were doing right then. We were establishing our code, our *modus operandi*, in this our first meeting and confrontation; our standards were being set. I would not lock the door. I knew if I locked it that first morning, it would be necessary to lock it each successive morning and afternoon—every time any of us went in or out. I did not want that. I wanted eventually to develop free access.

I did not think all this as I lay there on the floor: I just did not want to lock the door, and so I held on tight and said again softly, "Good morning, Chris. I'm glad to see you."

I inched my way across the floor, never looking up, until I had my back against the door. Then I let go of Chris's belt. He tore at the knob and rattled the door. I braced my feet on the tile floor and leaned my full weight against the door. At least, I thought, the man must be gone by now.

Chris stopped shaking the door and stood looking at me. Did he remember those times a year ago in Helga's class? I thought I saw a flicker in the huge gray eyes, but I could not be sure.

"Hiya, Chris," I say from the floor.

Momentarily he smiles, but it is so swift a smile that it ends long before it reaches his eyes. He moves back away from the door and for one long minute we look at each other—full, complete eye contact.

Then deliberately he takes off his coat and throws it on the floor. Is this what he always does and why there is no need for his name above a coat hook—or is he merely testing me?

I get up from the floor. "Hang it up, Chris."

He laughs and runs and so I go and get him. There is no point in calling to him: he will not come and I want to make words meaningful, and so I go and get him and a red crayon. There is no time to find labels and make neat lettering.

I lead him to the coat hooks and point to the hook farthest on the right.

"This is yours," I tell him. "This is where you will hang your coat."

He does not pull away from me now but stands silently as I write CHRIS in large red-crayon letters on the wall above the hook. Defacing church property? So be it.

"Get your coat, Chris. Hang it here."

Wrong. He laughs and runs again.

I go and get him once again and we go together to the center of the room where his discarded coat lies on the floor and I take his hand and guide it to the coat—but he will not pick it up and instead slumps slack and boneless to the floor, laughing his shrill laugh.

I prop him up, my hand closes over his, and we take the coat and hang it on the hook beneath his name.

"Good for you," I say.

But there is a tapping at the door and he does not even seem to hear me now. Instead, he finds two drumsticks in the wooden chest and takes them and climbs up on the jungle gym in the corner of the room, climbs until he reaches the highest platform— and there he folds his legs beneath him, and his mind inside him and his gray eyes look blankly down.

You are so small, I think. Seven years, and you cannot weigh more than fifty pounds. Your eyes seem bigger than the rest of you; they dominate your small, square face like diffuse gray clouds covering a sky. . . . But I have watched and I have seen you be aware; I remember when your eyes would clear, lit from behind—and I will have more of this.

I go to the door to investigate the tapping. A stout woman is there, holding a large, curly-haired boy in her arms.

"Miss MacCracken?" Her speech is cultured, almost English in articulation. "I understand that you will be filling in for Joyce. A tragic thing. Tragic. For her as well as for our poor children. Well, there's nothing to do but make the best of it."

She comes into the room, where Chris is beating a tattoo on the highest platform of the jungle gym, and stands the boy on the floor, takes off his red bonnet and mittens; then lays him on the floor and takes off his white shoes so that she can get the red snowsuit over his feet—unzips his overalls and feels inside his rubber pants.

"Oh, dear. He's wet again. Never mind, I'll fix it." And she changes him there on the floor.

Then she rises and hands me the plastic bag of diapers, first removing two baby bottles full of milk, complete with rubber nipples.

"I'll put these in the refrigerator for you, although I must say I don't think much of that refrigerator. It must be at least five years old—not even a separate freezer so the poor children can have ice cream. Still, we mustn't complain, must we? Now, the baby food is in the bag. It will be all right until you open the jars; then be sure to refrigerate it. Poor girl. It must be difficult for you to get the hang of things. Well, you can always call me. I'm never far from Bradford if he needs me."

She kisses him then and calls to Chris, "Good morning, Christopher. Have fun with Bradford."

She addresses me: "My, Christopher is athletic, isn't he? Climbing way up there. Well, each of us has our own strengths. And the boys Christopher and Bradford do have such a marvelous time together."

She left then before I could speak. Which was perhaps just as well. The only thing I could think to do was to look at Brad's folder; perhaps I would regain some semblance of reality.

There it was. Brad. Bradford Turner. I checked the birth date. He was six years old.

My God, I thought, what kind of a class is this?

I was to find out later that this was the most difficult class I would ever teach, the hardest, the lowest-functioning. Four untoilet-trained boys, three of whom were nonverbal, ranging in age from five to eight. But I was unschooled—and while I knew it was somewhat different from Helga's class, in my naïveté I thought, "Well, at least it's a challenge. In a way, I'm lucky—there's no way to go but up."

Then in my mind's ear I heard Helga's voice, "You sound like a shitty Pollyanna. Get to work." And I laughed out loud.

Louis was brought in by one of the women drivers and I recognized him immediately. If his name was not familiar to me, his blue football helmet was, and I remembered hearing the staff psychiatrist discussing him in Renée's room. There was discussion as to whether he should be placed in her room for the remaining days. This would be his last year at the school; he was having multiple seizures now, sometimes as many as four or five in one hour. While it was never stated in words, most of us were sure these were epileptic in nature.

There was nothing much to do for Louis now except make sure his small football helmet was securely fastened to protect his head, should he fall beyond reach, and to cover him until he woke again after an attack. He was staying on at the school only until his parents could find a suitable residential setting for him. Some of the staff thought that it was wrong to keep him on in a school designed for the emotionally disturbed—wrong for him and an imposition on the teachers who had not been trained, and did not want to give the kind of custodial care Louis needed. But the Director wanted him there.

His parents had been strong supporters of the school, grateful and willing helpers, and the Director felt a loyalty and a responsibility to help them now. And right or wrong, if the Director wanted him there, he stayed. So the problem had been temporarily resolved by moving Louis from Renée's room to Joyce's. Joyce was more tolerant, her room more removed, and Louis's unnamed but ever-increasing seizures were less noticeable and distracting to the other children and teachers. . . .

Louis's driver hands me his bib and an extra set of clothing and says, "Had a seizure on the way over. Went stiff—then right out—but he came to soon enough. Seems all right now."

I take off his hat and coat and he climbs upon the jumping-jack rocking horse and starts the motion that he will keep up all day unless he is lifted off— up and down, up and down—the springs beneath him groaning under the weight of his eight-year-old body. Saliva runs down his chin and I wipe it with the first of many Kleenexes and say, "Good morning, Louis," but his blue eyes do not focus and the motion does not stop—up and down, up and down. I wonder if there is such a thing as mental masturbation.

Someone crashes against the door and I open it to Tom, the boy who ran down the stairs so many eons ago when I was first searching for Helga's classroom. Tom is a tall, frail boy with wispy black hair falling across his eyes. All his shirts and sweaters have turtlenecks, which he unfolds and pulls up over his chin and eyes whenever a situation grows too threatening.

Tom has a bell in one hand; the other is behind his back. He emerges from the turtleneck, clangs the bell, and shouts, "Circle time!"

"Thank you," I answer. "Good morning, Tom."

"Good morning, Tom," he replies, and leaves us.

Circle time. The formal day at the school began with Circle each morning. It was the only time during the day when the Director observed all of us closely and noted the relationship between child and teacher, teacher and teacher, and improvements and lapses in each child. At the beginning of Circle we all sang to each child, singling him out, making him special, and on Wednesday afternoons at staff meetings there would be references to how the child acted. Group singing followed the individual greeting, and then the galloping and skating exercises and other games, which the Director said were designed for "gross motor development." These were followed by more social, nursery-school-type games where the children chose partners and again the Director watched for "peer relationships."

It was a warm and friendly time. Most teachers had aides assigned to them and the aides arrived as Circle began, so that the ratio of child to adult was two to one.

And now it is time, the first time, for me to take my own class to Circle. But so far there are only three children. Where is my other one? Billy. Well, perhaps his was one of the phone calls; perhaps the weather or a cold has kept him home.

I survey my three: Chris on the top of the jungle gym, Brad sitting placidly on the floor bulging like a Buddha because of his many diapers, Louis up-and-downing it on the rocking horse. How do I gather these three and get them down the long hall to the room where Circle is held?

I stand beside the jungle gym. "Circle time, Chris. Let's go."

He spreads himself flat and laughs his silver

laugh. I climb seven rungs until I can reach the platform, and then lift his slack body down beside me.
How can he be so heavy when he is so small? But at
least he does not seem inclined to run, and lets me
hold his hand. With the other hand I disentangle
Louis from the rocking horse and support him
against my side. Now Brad—how to get him there?
Lacking alternatives, I simply say once again, "Circle
time, Brad. Come on now." And surprisingly he
stirs. He rocks forward until he can push against the
floor with his hands, push himself up to a standing
position, and then he willingly waddles to me and
holds my skirt—and we are off down the hall toward
Circle.

The others are already there. Twelve more children; quite a few must be absent because I know
there are twenty-four children in the school, and five
other teachers, one for every four children. They call
across the room, introducing themselves to me—
Susan, small and blond; Renée; Carolyn, tall, black-
haired, beautiful; Ruth, red-haired with glasses; and
Dan, a new male teacher replacing Nick, blue eyes,
strong-looking in a khaki shirt. The Director smiles
from in front of the piano and I maneuver my three
to the small chairs in the Circle. The Director mo-
tions to a woman on the side of the room who comes
and sits next to Louis and so I put Brad and Chris
on either side of me.

The singing starts, all the teachers and some of
the children joining voices—the Director plays the
piano, leading us.

> "Good morning to you,
> Good morning to you,
> Good morning, dear Louis,
> We're glad to see you."

I reach across Brad and touch Louis's shoulder as we sing to him—the blue eyes are marbles, and the woman beside him wipes his chin.

We sing to Brad and I smile down at him and take his pudgy hand and touch his bulging stomach with it, and he beams up at me—brown curls, rosy cheeks, brown eyes, a beautiful child, but how can he manage to look only two years old when he is six? No time to think now. It's Chris's turn. He decides that he must leave his chair and sit on me—he winds his arm tight, tight, around my neck. From across the room it must look as though he's hugging me affectionately, and the teachers smile approvingly at this sign of rapport. Only I can feel his sharp fingernails as he pinches the skin below my ear, pinches hard, and I lift him back to his chair and my hand holds him there as we finish the song ... "Good morning, dear Chris, I'm glad to see you."

I soon saw why there had been no lesson plan. There was no one to do lessons. Nor was there time. The day was consumed with eating and eliminating. Circle took approximately forty-five minutes; when it was over, the classes went to the bathroom. My class changed its diapers. The Director told me this as the other children left the room and I nodded, still filing away the picture of that morning's Circle in my mind. It had not changed much since the first day I visited: although some of the children were different, they were still beautiful; although Helga was no longer there, the strength and the loving were.

As we made our slow trek back to our classroom, we passed the furnace room where Zoe, chief cook and bottle washer, secretary, public relations expert, and the Director's right hand, was beginning to heat a frozen casserole in the electric warming cart.

We were just rounding the corner, Chris and Louis holding my hands, Brad waddling behind, when I heard Zoe say, "Jesus, cut that out, Franklin!"

"Aw, come on, Zoe, one quick one. I never did it in a furnace room, did you?"

That must be that new teacher, I thought, Dan Franklin. Zoe called everybody by their last name.

"Go on, get out now. Quit kidding around." But there was laughter behind her voice.

"Okay. All right. I'll catch you later then. Incidentally, who's the new teacher with Joyce's class? Where'd she come from!"

"Came from the Junior League. One of the volunteers."

"The Junior League? You're kidding? Jeez! Well, Zoe, I'll bet 'Junior League' doesn't last a week. I'll lay a meatball on it."

"Okay, you're on, Franklin. She's better than you think. I saw her work with Helga last year."

Billy was my fourth child. He was the youngest in the class, just five, with blond, wavy hair and a soft, unformed face with a rosy, puckered mouth and, like the others, not toilet trained. His mother was young, separated from her husband, and she would bring Billy to school an hour or so late each morning. The Director spoke to her about this, then Dr. Steinmetz, the psychologist, finally Vic Marino, our psychiatrist, each explaining how important the schedule, the routine, was for Billy, how necessary the regular scheduling . . . and she would agree—and then the next morning come as late as usual—or later—dark, bruised hollows beneath her eyes.

It was hard not knowing what happened to the children when they left school. They did not speak, and so there was no way to learn from them.

Helga had been sure some of them were physically abused, and told me of visiting one family unannounced and finding the boy chained to a doghouse in the high-fenced backyard, his food and water on the ground.

But if some parents were cruel, others were kind and devoted, making unbelievable sacrifices for the special child within their home. Schizophrenic children are classically poor sleepers, refusing to go to bed, haunted by nightmares; and often the parents slept in shifts, keeping watch over the child who controlled their home. This schedule slowly eliminated sexual relations or even friendship between the parents. The children could be tyrants, and their houses could become filled with the hate common to tyranny.

To me the amazing thing was that the parents managed as well as they did—and that any teacher or outsider would presume to judge them. After all, we worked with the children five hours each day, from nine-thirty in the morning until two-thirty in the afternoon; but the parents were with them the other nineteen hours without surcease as they tried to care for their children and accomplish other chores as well. I felt compassion and admiration for their courage, and I often longed to reach out and put my arms around them as well as the children—not so much to care for them as to say what I could not put into words. I was not sure that I would have been as strong as they, had a child such as this been born to us. For more and more it seemed to me that there must be a chemical imbalance in at least some of these children—and who could say which ones?

But my job was not research. While I might hope for answers from the laboratories, still there was this day, this hour, when answers had not yet been found and my own job was teaching. I believed then and I believe still in the day school for emotionally disturbed children. There are valid reasons and occasions for residential settings, but whenever possible I believe the child is better at home with his parents. However, if the child is to go home to these parents each afternoon, then parent and teacher must try to work together.

And this was often difficult. To begin with, many of these parents had been hurt so often, lied to so much, accused of so many things, that their own defenses were high—or their own hopes had been abandoned and they had settled into what was easiest.

With Brad, for example, it was difficult for his mother to agree to leave the baby bottles and diapers home; and it was an important day for both of us when she brought me six pairs of white cotton training pants for him as a gift.

For I had set my goals. I was not a psychiatrist or even a trained teacher yet, but I was a mother and I had raised my own children. It seemed to me that if in those weeks while Joyce was absent I could teach the children to take care of their bodily needs—eat, go to the bathroom by themselves, dress themselves—and to communicate a little, I would have helped.

Zoe told me later how impossible my goals were—but because I was new, alone in my room at the far end of the hall, and had no one to tell me otherwise, I did not know it.

And so I bought five small plastic glasses and began. Each day after Circle we sat at the pink table and drank juice and ate cookies. At first they tipped over the glasses, dumped the juice upon the floor, threw the cookies; but they liked the sweet apple juice and the soft sugar cookies, and I would not let them have them unless they sat with me at the table. I wanted them to get the feeling of having a place where they felt safe. I knew no better way than to feed them there.

We also stripped. There alone in our bare class-room I took off their clothes. Not Louis—even I knew that he had left us, was now beyond reaching. But I took off the clothes of the other three piece by piece and taught them to put them back on by them-selves. For a half hour or more each morning we worked on learning to get dressed and undressed. I took off three pairs of shoes, three pairs of jeans, three pairs of diapers. I laid out three pairs of cotton training pants—one on Brad's chair, one on Billy's, one on Chris's. I worked with whichever one I could capture first, sitting him on the floor in front of his chair, guiding his hand to the underpants, then pushing him forward, laying the pants out on the floor in front of him, then bending first the right leg, aiming the right foot for the proper hole, then the left leg.

Standing him up, I'd hook his thumbs beneath the elastic at the top of the underpants and pull them up, and then, finally, I'd release the child and cap-ture another and begin again.

And somehow, it did not seem like drudgery. I was, after all, in bodily contact with the child the whole time, touching him, helping him learn. And I knew, without really knowing it, that this touching was my own best way of communicating with these children. There are other ways for other people, but I could almost hear the children through my finger-tips, and I think I also spoke to them.

That was all I asked for in the beginning, just the underpants. But I did not set our table or pour the juice until all the underpants were on.

For Chris, this was merely relearning. I had seen him put on and take off his own jacket, even his shoes, dozens of times in Helga's classroom. I knew he had not "regressed"; there was too much intelligence in his laughter, in his willful disobedience. It was a matter of getting through again.

Brad learned to manage both underpants and jeans—he could not get past his stomach to his shoes and socks.

Billy was much slower, finally able to pull on his underpants with help. I never got as far as taking off his shirt.

I was happy and totally absorbed. I loved being on my own with the children; they were making progress, I was sure of it—and now I understood Helga's reaction to having volunteers. I was glad the Director did not visit my room, grateful that no volunteer or aide had been assigned to us—just the children and myself. Without interference of adult words in the room, I could hear the unspoken words of the children—their rage, their refusals, their protests, their pleas, their questions, compliance, or excitement.

I stopped taking the class to the lunchroom for the noon meal. There they had been allowed to eat what they liked, Chris roaming around, snatching food from other plates. It was not that the school or Joyce was lax: I felt then and I still feel that of all the schools I've seen—and there have been quite a few now—ours was one of the finest. It was not that they were lax; it was that these four children of Joyce's were so difficult. They were in many ways more like small animals—some wild, some tame—than like human children. Because the other children in the school were more advanced, though perhaps as sick in their own way, the other teachers were more tolerant of these four. Asking less, making fewer demands.

But I did not want this. If I accepted it, or allowed the children to, it meant that I did not believe they could improve; and if this was so then we were without hope. And it was nceessary to hope; more than necessary—it was essential. On this I built my own new creed. I believed in the children.

I had tried teaching them to eat sitting in the lunchroom. But it was too difficult. The day in my second week that I tried to keep Chris in his chair at lunch, I could not. He performed his trick of turning his small body into a limp, heavy weight, and slid from his chair to lie beneath the table on the floor; and when I reached down to retrieve him, he set his teeth into my hand and bit so hard that I had to pull it back.

And Brad wept for his bottle and Billy howled and the other teachers were uncomfortable with the commotion.

Dan spoke to me about it after school. He found me in my classroom long after the children had gone home. He came in, turned one of the small pink chairs backward, straddling it, and studied me with his blue eyes.

"That was a rough scene today. How's your hand?"

He was too big in my classroom. Incongruous with the pale green wall and tiny chairs. He was well over six feet tall, and now his long legs stretched out interminably across the tile floor. His remarks to Zoe still burned in my ears and I wished only that he would leave.

"Fine, thanks. Nothing at all."

But his hand insists, examines the purple swelling, touching it with his fingertips. "No skin broken. That's good," he says.

I pull away, conscious of his youth, of the maleness of him, and go to wash my blackboard. If he notices he doesn't show it, and goes on talking in his slow way, actually helping me devise a plan

whereby my class can eat in our own room. He be-
lieves my boys can learn to eat like other children
and I am grateful to him for this.

They were learning to feed themselves, to dress
themselves; but still they were not toilet-trained. It
had never been a problem with Elizabeth or Rick,
and sometimes I had felt that some of my friends
were overanxious concerning their own children's
early toilet training. But here in school it was different; these children were five, six, seven—Louis was
eight, but I did not try to change him; it would have
been cruel and useless. But I was sure that the others could learn to go to the bathroom in a toilet
rather than in their diapers—and if they could learn
to do this, perhaps their parents could take them
with them on small trips or at least feel some pride
and relief, and maybe hope, in their children. I
wanted this, because if I had an enemy, if I did battle against any one thing while I was at the school, it
was against the "institution."

There were some good residential settings, but the
cost was exorbitant—over seven thousand dollars a
year even then. And I had seen some of the others—
the state institutions for the mentally ill where the
children were mixed with the adults and wore only
hospital gowns and dropped their feces upon the
floor. I had read and heard tales of horror, and I
fought hard to keep the children from being sent
there. Every time I had to change a diaper or mop
the excrement from my classroom floor, I fought a
little harder, worked more determinedly, to train my
children.

Dan suggested that I speak to the Director about
having the children eat lunch in our room rather
than in the lunchroom. He felt that she would wel-

come the relief from the bedlam my four created, as
long as I was willing to undertake it alone. And he
was right.

So each day after that, Zoe would bring our share
of the casserole, milk, and dessert on a tray and hand
it to me at the door. I would set our table with mats
and paper napkins from the five-and-ten and our
plastic glasses and paper bowls. None of these children had eating problems in a classical sense; these
four were all hungry; there was no difficulty in swallowing, no anorexia—they just had not learned how
to eat.

I served each of us a small portion from the large
casserole into the separate bowls, and as long as the
child stayed at the table he could eat. I would not
permit him to carry his bowl to a corner or, as Chris
wished, to the platform of the jungle gym. We ate
together at the table—ate our casserole, our dessert,
drank our milk. At first they ate with their fingers,
then when I thought they were ready I gave them
spoons and insisted they use these instead of fingers.
In the beginning I used my own fingers, then when I
gave them spoons, I used one myself so that they
could see me, could have a live model to watch
closely, to imitate. It is a tricky thing, getting food
onto a spoon, carrying it to your face and putting it
in the right hole without being able to see what you
are doing. It takes practice; it also helps if you can
actually see someone else doing it. See that it is possible. It was not that they had never seen people eat
at a table before or use silverware; it was just that I
believed that in order to learn to do something you
had to understand it and you had to want to do it. I
tried to break each task into its smallest segments,
teaching first one part and then the next, building
on each tiny success.

Chris could do, had done, many of these things before. He had once been toilet-trained, once had eaten at a table; I had an advantage here because I had seen him with Helga and I knew he was capable of it. But he refused. Willfully he dumped food, knocked over his chair, peed on the floor—as if deliberately trying to anger or test me—laughing all the while. Yet there was fear inside him; I could feel it when I touched him, feel it gradually go out as I held him and he realized I wouldn't hurt him. I remembered the farm across the road, summers when I was small, where they bred riding horses. I remembered the wild kicking and bucking when the saddle first went on—and the gradual gentling. I was trying to gentle Chris.

His parents were close to giving up. They loved him, but the father would come in in the morning and sit awhile now, and sometimes he would begin to tell me of the night before. Then I would motion him into the hall where we could talk, watching Chris through the window in the door—the unlocked door. He was pleased with that, and nice enough to tell me. He remembered well that first morning, with me flat on the floor while he watched me from this same window, and we laughed together over that.

At home they locked things too. They now had a padlock on a drawer in the kitchen. Ever since they had found the crib slashed. Chris's brother was four months old now, and one morning they had gone into his room to find the mattress cut open in a dozen places, the baby still in the crib—and Chris there with the knife, laughing. His father took the knife and all the others in the house and locked them in the kitchen drawer, and Chris's mother wore the key on a string around her neck. The carving set was too large for the drawer; they hid that under the mattress of their double bed.

It was a terrible thing, a terrible way to live, and I could not censure them. They were pleased, though, that Chris no longer needed to be locked in the classroom: perhaps sometime other locks could be opened.

Brad was very different. Eager to copy, eager to please, he followed me everywhere, learning so fast that it was difficult to keep up with him. The world delighted him, beginning with his own fat stomach, which he now could see as he pulled on his underpants and shirt. He patted it with proud satisfaction and repeated the word "Brad." He was discovering himself; what's more, there was a name. There was a name for everything: nose, mouth, eyes. Point to it, name it. Often he doubled the word; if he particularly liked something it became "cup-cup" or "ball-ball." I was pleased to be "Mair-Mair."

It was hard to understand why he hadn't talked before. I brought it up at staff meeting, but no one seemed to know or would say. It was difficult for the staff—psychologist, psychiatrist, speech therapist, psychiatric social worker—impressive names and for the most part competent people—but they were there only one day a week. The budget would not allow for more, the Director said, and I'm sure this was true; also, she was saving for her dream: a new school, not rented or borrowed, but built specifically for these children—her school. It was her dream, and now with her husband dead and her only son married it became her life.

In any event, the professionals came only on Wednesday, and most for only half a day or less, and there were twenty-four children. So it was difficult for them to see every child weekly, and understandable that they would hesitate to commit themselves. Yet who else could help?

Eventually, teachers did evolve their own answers, knowing they were speculations, subject to error. But as they searched for solutions to a child's problem, they were forced to consider causes and motivations and they did develop personal, private theories.

In Brad's case, he was bright and beautiful but infantile. In a way, it seemed as if he had been kept this way, as if he should remain a perennial infant. He had one sister, seventeen years old; both parents were in their late forties. His father was president of a large insurance company; both parents had advanced degrees.

I do not think his mother consciously wished to keep Brad from learning to speak, but his babyish ways and dependence on her were essential to her, making her feel needed. Still, I think he had not spoken primarily because he had never needed to speak. Everything was provided for him, his wishes anticipated, his wants satisfied, before he asked. He lay like a fat, comfy king, satiated and full without lifting his finger, much less his tongue, while words gushed over him. He didn't realize that words had a specific meaning; instead, they were only pleasant sounds, his mother's speech so fluent and verbose that it was meaningless to him. So now it was interesting to learn that things and people had names; to discover that he could make things happen through speech was exciting. If he said "water," or an approximation thereof, he got water. It was worthwhile to learn and use these words.

It was interesting to watch the interrelationships between the boys begin to develop. Chris watched Brad. Brad was a better teacher for Chris than I was. I was an adult, and somewhat suspect. I might force my ways upon him—indeed, I had and did. But Brad was something new; Brad imitated me and gradually Chris imitated Brad. I laughed out loud one day when Chris got his shirt on over his head. He wore it for a half hour, without poking his head through, then finally it appeared. Brad patted him as soon as I did, saying, "Gu for you!"

The toilet training was the hardest. I took them all at regular intervals to the toilet. I still had to change Louis' diapers, which made it more difficult; but I would take each of the other three to the bathroom, staggering the times, hoping we would have it to ourselves. We used the girls' bathroom, and it was a typical Sunday-school setup—two sinks, three cubicles with toilets, a large counter with a wide mirror. We went to the bathroom many times a day, without success—they would wet their pants as soon as we returned to the classroom.

I bought a small chair potty and put it in the classroom, thinking immediacy might help. But it, too, was unsuccessful.

Finally I made a new decision. The way the children had learned to eat and begin to speak was by watching me, imitating me. I decided that perhaps this might also be true of peeing. Brad at least had probably never seen it done—nor Billy. Louis was without control; Chris was full of it. A small pun. Full of control and pee. He could go all day and never urinate, withholding it carefully unless he wished to let it go. Once he made an enormous puddle on the foot of a potential fund raiser. After that visitors to our classroom decreased even more.

I waited until the rest of the school was at the playground; I had made our excuses for remaining at school. Then I took the boys with me down the long hall into the bathroom, our voices echoing in the tiled emptiness. I propped open the door of one of the cubicles with the bench from the counter and, leaving the three outside the cubicle, went in, sat down on the toilet, and peed. They were fascinated. I was sorry I could not do it standing up—but at least they were interested.

"Now you," I said.

All the time I had been going I had said, "See the pee. Good. That's pee. That's good. Pee. Pee."

Brad took my place. He sat down on the toilet and looked between his fat legs.

"Pee?" he asked.

Nothing happened. Then a drop. Then a stream.

"Pee-pee. Brad's pee-pee," he shouted in delight.

"Good, good!" I said. "Pee in the toilet. Good." We were both undilutedly happy. I helped Brad off the seat and he put his pants back on. Then Chris pushed by us.

I bent forward to help him, but something told me to wait, to let him do it his own way. Chris turned his back to us, let down his pants, and stood in front of the toilet, his buttocks skinny, pale, vulnerable. Stood a minute—two—three—four—and then it came . . . a torrent. Not only was Chris peeing; he remembered how to do it like a boy; now he could show Brad. He turned and smiled at us when he was through, still holding his small penis, shaking it as though to extract every drop. He smiled, smiled without the usual accompanying mirthless laugh, and said, "I peed."

It took Billy longer; he was absent so much. But he had two good examples now, and three weeks later all three were peeing with pride, though Billy still covered his ears when the toilet flushed.

Friday of that week the Director came to my classroom and asked me to come to her office after school.

I dreaded going to see her—I had been there twelve weeks. I knew that Joyce must be ready to come back, that this was what she wanted to tell me. I was glad Joyce had recovered; but oh, if I could just have had a little longer, a little more time. There was so much more I wanted to do. We were working hard on language now that other things took less time, and this was a fascinating area—communication—I wanted more.

Ah, but I had had my chance. It had been good. I had no reason to complain. I walked quietly down the hall to the office that Friday afternoon.

We were alone, the Director and myself.

"You've done a good job, Mary," she said. "I'm pleased you could be here with us. I don't know what we would have done without you. The boys have been happy with you. I'm sure they would have progressed just as well with Joyce, but nonetheless they have not regressed. And you should be proud of that."

"Thank you," I said, feeling somehow sad. What was the matter with me? What did I want—accolades?

"Joyce will be back on Tuesday. I wanted to tell you so that you can say good-bye to the boys and collect your things."

"Oh, I don't need them," I said. What use did I have for five small plastic cups, rubber balls, scrapbooks? Whom would I show a picture to, saying, "Can you see the boy, Chris? Point to the boy . . ."

"Please keep them here. Perhaps Joyce will have some use for them." Tears were very close behind my eyes and I was eager to go. "Thank you for letting me come," I said and turned to go.

"Mary"—the Director's voice was brisk—"would you like to continue?"

"Continue . . . ?"

"Yes, keep on teaching here. Of course you should take some courses, but the need for teachers is desperate and we have an extremely long waiting list of children. I have been thinking about it, and I think perhaps we could clear out the storeroom opposite Dan's room and you could use that. It's small, but there are only about two months of school left and I think we could manage."

I couldn't believe it. My whole insides were singing.

"Yes," I said, "I'd like that. I'm sure we could manage."

You fraud. You fake. Oh, Mary, you phony. Think you could manage? You could manage on a pinhead if they'd let you come back—cool, calm, collected—how are you going to keep from bursting?

"Well, then," the Director said, "that's settled. On Monday you can pack up your things, and then the remainder of the week you can clear out the storeroom and get settled. I'll call the Norfolk School District and tell them we have an opening. I think what we'll do is add the children one at a time. That will give you a chance to get to know each one."

I hope I walked out the door. I can't remember it at all, or walking up the stairs or out the front door to my car. I only remember colliding with Dan.

"What did she say? What'd the old bat say?" Dan was not fond of the Director.

I told him, stumbling over words in my excitement, unable to contain myself.

Dan leaned against his Volkswagen and grinned. "Well, Junior League, I guess I owe Zoe a meatball."

"I heard that conversation."

"No kidding? Figured it might make you fight a little harder. Well, babe, I'll tell you one thing: you're the best teacher they've got and the old lady knows it. What salary did she offer you?"

"She didn't. I don't know. I didn't ask."

"Ohhh, Mary. For Pete's sake. Be careful. She

hangs on to her money as tight as she can! ... Regressed! Can't believe she said they hadn't regressed, although that was probably to keep you from asking for more salary. Haven't regressed. Jesus—they've only improved five and a half million per cent."

"Ah, Dan, thank you. I'm going to have my own class; can you believe it?"

"I not only believe it, Junior; I'm betting all my meatballs on you."

Chapter *SIX*

On Monday I told the boys that Joyce would be back the next day. I had spent a large part of the weekend thinking about how best to tell them. It was not that I was indispensable to them; it was just that we had started something together, and I did not want them to think that I had left without a reason or because of something they had done.

I decided to show them where I was going, and we walked down the hall and inspected the storeroom.

We spent the rest of the day cleaning out the room, packing books in boxes, carrying old magazines to the church secretary. The children pulled out as many books as they put in and accidentally tore some pages of the magazines. We did not get much accomplished, but I hoped they understood, through the doing, where I would be.

We said good-bye that afternoon. Chris, Brad, Billy, Louis. I would never forget them, nor the look and smell of that classroom—my first class, or if not my own, at least borrowed for a little while. We had learned a lot together. We had changed each other's lives more in those twelve weeks than most people do in a lifetime.

It seems so strange to me, now, that I know only a paragraph of information about the rest of their lives after we had such an intimate time together. Occasionally Chris and Brad would run to me at the playground and put their heads against my knee, but I was never in that back L-shaped room again

There was inside of me, of all of us teaching there, an instinctive knowledge of the necessity of letting go. When a child moved outside our immediate orbit we did not try to pursue him. I could not keep from asking Joyce, however, and I learned from her at the end of the year that a suitable place had been found for Louis, that Brad had continued to improve and would enter public school in the fall, that Chris's family moved South, and that Billy and his mother quietly disappeared during the early summer.

I keep my pictures, though, and my slides, in a carousel inside my head, and they will remain a part of me forever.

There was a four-day hiatus for me now. I cleaned the storeroom, and on Thursday I painted it pale yellow and polished the floor. After school on Friday, Dan helped me move in the tables, chairs, and bookcase that the Director had bought at a second-hand store. It was a tiny room, but its window faced east and the morning sun was clear and warming now with the beginning of spring.

After I had gone home, Dan bought a plant and put it on the windowsill in my room. I found it there on Monday morning when I came in. The card said only, "Every teacher needs a plant to water." It didn't need a signature.

Chapter SEVEN

Brian didn't come and didn't come, and I could not understand it. I had gotten there early on Monday morning, eager to see my first child, waiting for him, filled with excitement, anticipation. The Director had told me his name: Brian O'Connell, from the Norfolk School District. She had done an intake on him earlier and said that he was eight and had been kept at home because the public school system did not have a suitable place for him and that more complete records would follow. This was often the case, but I didn't care. I really wanted to meet him first anyway and form my own opinion.

He was to be sent by taxi that first morning; meanwhile, bussing would be worked out for him. I waited in the Director's office by the window, watching each car arrive, so that I would be there when he came.

But the final car came and went and still no Brian. I lingered in the office.

"What do you think, Zoe? What do you think happened? Do you think they changed their minds?"

"The fool taxi driver probably got lost. Do you want me to check the cab companies?"

Zoe had little respect for taxi and bus drivers, and she directed them like a diminutive traffic cop, morning and afternoon, as they transported the children, keeping them parked so that the traffic could flow, moving them on as soon as the child was safe, giving them hell if they were late. She would have tackled the entire Norfolk cab line if I had asked her to. Loyal, snappy—if Zoe liked you she could never help enough; if she didn't, you could court her endlessly without winning a glance.

Perhaps the driver *had* gotten lost. Zoe was often right, and I listened to her pithy wisdom as much as to the words of the professionals. Still, a call to the cab companies might prompt a call to the school district—and I didn't want an emergency alarm the first day.

"I think I'll go outside and wait a few more minutes," I told her.

Down to my classroom, past the Circle room, where I could hear the strains of "Here we go, Looby-Loo," and I knew Dan would be gritting his teeth as he sang. He hated Circle, considering the songs and games too childish for his boys. I took my coat from the hook marked MARY. There had been time to make the labels for this room—so far we had only two: MARY and BRIAN.

Outside, spring was beginning again. It always made itself known so urgently. Summer, fall, winter, did not impress themselves on my senses quite so ardently, but spring could never be ignored. The grounds surrounding the church were beautiful. There were two gardeners, so everything was carefully maintained. Just now there were crocuses and the beginning shoots of jonquils and daffodils, and forsythia spilled across the edges of the black macadam drive, softening its appearance.

It was a long sloping driveway, curving from the large parking lot at the side around to the back. It was in the back that the drivers let the children out, by the Director's office. I waited there awhile and then, feeling the wind, started to walk in order to warm myself.

The church itself was new, modern, handsome, in design. The building holding the Sunday-school rooms, the minister's office, and so forth, was open and large. It was here that we had our classes. I walked around it now, admiring the flow of line, the sensitive use of wood and stone, the windows, the recessed doorways.

I stopped suddenly in front of one of the doorways. There was a small figure crouched on the steps. I moved closer and saw it was a boy who arched and stared, instantly, totally still, much like a deer at unexpected sound or sight. I had the feeling that he might bolt if I approached too suddenly.

I waved to him and walked on a little way, then turned and walked back past him, calling to him this time, "Good morning." There was a flurry of movement at my voice, but he did not leave the step. I went on past but zigzagged my parallel tracks so that I came closer to the steps.

He was wearing gray pants, a gray peaked cap pulled low over his eyes, a blue plaid jacket with a piece of white paper pinned to one shoulder with a safety pin. Written on it were two words: *Brian O'Connell.*

I stopped in front of him. "Hello, Brian," I said. His arms began to flap up and down in rapid motion. He reminded me now of a wounded bird, desperate to fly away but unable to leave the ground.

Why would they pin his name on him? Was he unable to remember it—or unable to speak?

"I'm Mary," I said, speaking slowly, softly, my voice just above a whisper. "I'm your teacher. I'm glad you're here."

What a hell of a way for him to arrive. What a horrible way to start school. The driver must have been new, must have let him out at the wrong door, and he had simply huddled there. Thank God he had not run. I was not sure how to get him inside. I talked a little more, softly, waiting to get an idea or a feel of what was best to do.

But we could not stay there much longer. Soon someone would come out, the Director, Zoe ... additional people would frighten him even more.

I moved closer to him and the flapping started again, wildly, then slowed. I wondered if I dared to touch him. Not yet. It was not right yet. But I could see him shivering, even with his heavy jacket.

It was time to go in.

"Come," I said, "it's time for school to begin." And I led off, slowly, willing him to follow.

As it happened, I was lucky. I had chanced upon one of the best motivators for Brian: curiosity. I found out later that he was a naturally curious child, eager, bright; he was often triggered into trying something new because of his overwhelming desire to know.

Back up the macadam drive, avoiding the Director's office. That would be too much for him now. Into a small side door. I walked quickly, hoping to reach our classroom before Circle ended, pacing my walk to the sound of his steps, trying never to get too far in front for fear of losing him, but trying to move quickly.

Into the school, down the short flight of steps—my classroom was the first on the right. Good—I had left the door open. No need to pause. Into the room, and he followed. I shut the door then—not to keep him there but to soften some of the noise as the others burst from the Circle room.

"This is our room," I said. "This is where I hang my coat."

I pointed to the other hook, the one with BRIAN neatly labeled over it. "This is where you hang yours."

The flapping was just in the hands now. He circled the perimeter of the room, letting his hands flutter against the walls. I knew the feeling; often I had wanted to do it myself at large parties, to know the beginning and the end, to orient myself in relation to the periphery.

I sat down and let him flutter by. There was no hurry. I moved one of the small chairs over to the window and sat in the sunlight, looking toward the door. Keeping watch so that I could warn him, soften the surprise if the Director or someone were to come in.

Dan's face appeared in the window of the doorway. I smiled to show him that all was well, and signaled that we needed time. He waved back and gave the okay sign—thumb and forefinger together, last three fingers raised.

I knew we were all right then. Dan would tell Zoe that Brian had arrived and would explain to the Director, if she was there, though often she left right after Circle to make a fund-raising speech or do a screening interview.

For almost an hour Brian walked our room, paced its length and breadth, in the beginning making large detours around me, making the loop smaller and smaller until now he passed within twelve inches of me.

I talked to him from time to time—about the school, where the bathroom was, how many children were there, where we ate lunch. It was like singing, more like singing than talking, really—like the songs I used to sing to Elizabeth and Rick when they were small and ill with measles or chicken pox and would wake whimpering in the night. I would sit on the end of their beds and sing all the songs I could remember, the songs my mother had sung to me, camp songs, college songs, love songs; the content did not matter, nor the fact that my voice was funny and off-key. It was a way of telling them that I was there, so that they could relax and sleep again and not need to keep opening their eyes or cry or ask questions they didn't want answered. As long as they could hear my voice, there was no need to check.

It was the same now. I talked to Brian to give him the feeling of safety, to remove his fear.

He came closer and closer, never speaking himself, until finally he slowed to a stop in front of me.

Now it was right. Now I could touch him. I reached toward his shoulder and unpinned the white paper from his jacket. This touch was light, light—merely the unfastening of a pin—but a beginning; we had made contact.

"You don't need this anymore," I said. "I know your name."

He stood so still; his skin pale, nose and cheeks sprinkled with freckles, green eyes with black centers and long black lashes never flickering from mine.

Then he left me—twice more around the room, then diagonally across to the center ... around again ... back in front of me for another long look. Then to the coat hooks. He stood there a long time. Around the room, back to the coat hooks. He touched my coat, touched it so quickly it was almost an illusion. Around the room to in front of me. So close his legs almost touched my knees.

I know what he wants now. He wants to stay. Stay here. But what is the trouble? Something—something more. Ah, the buttons. He cannot manage the buttons on his jacket.

There are four. Large black buttons. And I start with the one at the bottom—easier for him than to have my hands too near his face, his throat, in the beginning. I move up the middle, finally the last button is undone and back he goes to the coat hook. A flutter now. Back to me ... more flutter. Ah, but this I won't do for him. He is eight; he should be able to take off his coat.

The fluttering builds and builds and I say, "All right now; I'll start one sleeve," and I tug gently at the right sleeve of his jacket until it is away from his shoulder and the arm is almost out.

Back he goes to the coat hook—flapping, wiggling, flapping, until he gets it off—and the jacket falls against the floor.

I watch quietly, quietly, never moving from my chair. And he leans down and picks it up and hangs it on the hook beneath his name.

It is almost lunchtime. I am sure now and I move without hesitating. What is it? How do I know that I cannot lose him now? He has yet to speak, and yet I know with utmost surety that I am home free.

I hear noises in the hall and I say to Brian, "It's time for lunch. Let's go wash."

I take his hand and walk down the hall, depositing him outside the boys' bathroom without a qualm.

"I'll wait for you here," I say, and when he comes out I note with delight his unzipped pants. No toilet training needed here.

"Zipper up," I say. And he looks down at his pants and solemnly pulls up the zipper.

But in the lunchroom he panics. I sit beside him, and even though we are not directly touching I can feel his whole body trembling. They serve his plate, and his arms begin to flap. Unmeaningly his flapping arm knocks a tray of paper cups filled with milk from Zoe's hands.

"Shit," she says.

Brian runs, screaming, flapping. Around the lunchroom, unable to find the door, bumping blindly into chairs, other children.

"Awk—awk," he goes. Some strange, strangled cry, "Awwwwkkk—awwwwwwwwwkkk," more like a dying chicken than a boy.

I get up and gently capture him and lead him from the room, and as we go out the door he speaks, or rather screams in terror, his first words.

"Gonna go to the doctor's! Awwwwwkk. Awwwwwkk. Gonna go to the doctor's!"

Back in our room, I hold him on my lap. We are both a little too big, a little too old, for the chair, but we have a need for it.

"Now, what is this?" I say. "What is all this yelling, screaming, about the doctor? There are no doctors here." Mentally I apologize to our psychiatrist. "We do not have time for doctor's visits when we are at school. Doctors are all right, but we are too busy here for them. We have too much to do, you and I, too much to see, to learn, to have time for doctors."

Again my words do not matter. I use them as a means to drive away his terror. Inch by slow inch I can feel the fear go and, sitting on the chair still holding him, I sing Helga's old song, "Camptown races all day long—do dah, do dah. Camptown races, hear my song—all the do dah day."

As his body relaxes, I let my thoughts drift. Why was he so frightened? Was it the other children? No. It was the food. It was when they served his food that the real panic came. And what doctor? Why had he screamed that? Had he been hospitalized? Or merely threatened?

Now I needed those charts, those records. I hoped the Director would get them quickly.

Chapter EIGHT

It was two weeks before the records came. I searched them carefully, but there was no mention of hospitalization. There was a transcript of an interview that the parents had had at a mental health clinic. Brian was an only child. The father was described as intelligent, aggressive; the mother as slender, pretty, extremely nervous. He was the top man in a small wholesale grocery. Both parents said there had never been any trouble with Brian; both were described by the social worker as somewhat uncooperative.

The psychologist reported that it had been impossible to examine Brian; he had run screaming around the office during the entire testing period; his summation read "Impossible to evaluate." A social worker had interviewed Brian's mother, who said that pregnancy and birth had both been normal; she thought the trouble had begun when she had gone to work, helping out at a local health spa, and sent Brian to an all-day nursery. She said that they had abused him there, that he had been fine until then. But when she was asked the date of Brian's birth, she gave her own birth date. When she was asked her own, she gave his. When Brian was brought in to join his mother after the unsuccessful psychological testing, he had climbed on her lap and settled into the nursing position and then lay quietly. The social worker noted that there was a symbiotic relationship between mother and son.

I put the folder back in the file. There seemed to be so much blame. What good was that? Blame produced guilt, and guilt, hostility; there was no growth in that.

Brian's mother came to school with him on the second day. She arrived in the taxi with Brian and, unasked, uninvited, she settled herself in our room. She was thin, fragile-looking, and talked without stopping. Her fingers picked nervously at her nylon-knit turquoise dress as she chattered on and on.

Brian ran the whole morning. He fluttered so hard he seemed palsied. By eleven o'clock I could take no more.

"Excuse me," I said. And went to look for Zoe. The rapport that Brian and I had begun to build was leaking out of the room; I could feel it go.

I found Zoe in the furnace room heating up the casserole for lunch on a covered electric hot tray.

"Guess what's for lunch today! Same thing as last Tuesday, Wednesday, and Friday: cut-up hot dogs in canned baked beans. Only today it's frozen solid. The church ladies who brought it said they'd made it last week and then forgot to take it out of the freezer last night. I told them I understood. Anybody knows it takes so much time to cut up twelve hot dogs you have to do it a week ahead of time. Particularly, if there're only five of you . . . What's the matter?"

"Zoe, can you get Mrs. O'Connell to leave my room for a little while? She's been there all morning. Brian's so nervous he's climbing the walls. And I'm about to follow . . ."

Zoe strode out of the furnace room, hiking up her skirt on her five-foot body. She opened the door to my room.

"Mrs. O'Connell, I need your help with lunch. Now!"

And Mrs. O'Connell followed Zoe obediently.

I took my chair to the window, and this time Brian also brought a chair and sat there beside me. I got up and brought back a wooden puzzle—only four pieces. I dumped them out and idly began to put them back in place. Deliberately, I maneuvered the fourth piece in backward, pushing at it, unable to make it fit. Then, sighing, I pushed it away, put it on the windowsill, just beyond Brian's reach.

My thoughts turned back to Mrs. O'Connell. Foolish, foolish I was to be annoyed by her. I must learn more patience. It was a windfall, really, to have her here. I should take advantage of the fact, use it, find out more. I needed her as an ally. The enemy I fought was too large to defeat alone. I could not keep the children from the institution by myself; I needed help. And what better help than from the parents? Those who had borne him, fed him, cared for him, and loved him. I saw again the room at an institution I had visited: there was no love there, only the revolting smell of Clorox mixed with urine and excrement. I repented my sin of omission. After lunch I would invite her back and see if we could try to hear each other.

Ahhhh now, look at Brian. He cannot resist that puzzle. He moves his chair closer to the windowsill and looks quickly at me to see if I watch him—but I stare sleepily out the window. Feeling safe, he takes his index finger, the same hand that could not unbutton a jacket, and with a quick, deft movement he spins the missing piece into place. I feel delight pulse in me—I do not think that there is any retardation here. Careful, though. It is too soon to praise. I long to get up and get another puzzle, one with five pieces, perhaps six. But I hold myself in check and keep my mock sleepiness turned toward the window.

Mrs. O'Connell reappears in the doorway, gets her purse from the shelf, brings it to me and takes out a bottle of red liquid.

"Brian's medicine," she says.

"Oh," I say, "what is it for?"—thinking perhaps a cold.

She leans close to whisper: "Stops the fits."

"Fits?"

"Yes. You know"—and she flaps in perfect imitation.

The Director has not mentioned medication—how am I to find out all that I need to know?

"Do you think we could talk a little more after lunch?" I ask. "The children usually rest then for a half hour. If Zoe came down and stayed with Brian, could we talk?"

There is the same startled look that I have seen in Brian's eyes, but dulled, glazed.

"Lunch?" she says, "Brian doesn't eat lunch. He doesn't like to eat."

"Oh," I say, "why is that?"

"I don't know. Maybe it was the nursery school. I shouldn't have worked, shouldn't have sent him there. But Jack was never home, and I—there was nothing . . ." Quickly she stops.

"Did he eat before?" I ask.

"Oh yes. He nursed like a little pig—and he loved the puddings and the applesauce."

Oh, God, I think. Only soft foods. And now he's eight. Eight. I can feel impatience begin to grow in me again; there is so little time left.

"What does he eat now?" I ask. "At home, I mean."

"Same as he does anywhere. We take it with us when we eat at Gramma's. See, I brought it here."

She brings a paper bag from the shelf above the hooks. She opens it and hands me a large box of saltines and a jar of powdered chocolate. I read the label: an instant chocolate-milk drink.

"A snack?" I say, knowing it isn't—only hoping. "He likes this for a snack?"

She says it for me, blunt and clear. "That's what he eats. That's all he eats. That's all he's eaten since he was four."

Chapter *NINE*

We discussed it at staff. I wrote out a report on Brian's eating, also the incident of medication, and read it at staff meeting. Read it so the subject could not be diluted or diverted. I needed advice. This was a medical problem, and I was out of my depth. Could a child live on only saltines and chocolate milk? It seemed unlikely to me, but to get Brian to eat anything else would be a major problem and I might alienate him altogether.

There was some discussion. Dr. Marino, our psychiatrist, who was, of course, an M.D., said he doubted that a child's body could develop normally on such a diet, adding that it did not sound like true anorexia in that the child was evidently not starving himself—actually, he was quite plump.

"Let's see how it goes," Marino said. "We can discuss it again in a couple of weeks."

"We'll leave it up to you, Mary," added the Director. "You can keep us filled in."

How can you leave it up to me when I know nothing? Nothing. Frustration and weariness pile upon me. Five experts in the room, at approximately thirty dollars an hour. We sit around this table, at this meeting, for two hours—sixty dollars times five means three hundred dollars for our professionals this afternoon—and they decide to leave it up to me.

The discussion has already left Brian, is focusing on Gene Spencer's penchant for biting. All right.

Okay. What we seem to have here is do-it-yourself therapy. All the books I've studied warn the teacher against playing psychiatrist. Good. Right. But suppose nobody else will play? Then what? Then what remains are teacher's guesses. And the phrase "uneducated guess" rings in my ears.

Driving home, I have a small consultation with myself and decide that since there are only six weeks left before summer I will ask only that Brian sit quietly with me at the table during the lunch hour. He will be served the same food as the other children—no special chocolate milk or crackers—but he can eat or drink whatever he pleases. He will not be forced or even urged to eat. Hopefully, his own hunger will provide the impetus for eating once his panic subsides.

Dr. Marino did check on the medication, calling the family doctor who had prescribed it. A mild tranquilizer. Yes, it could be discontinued in school —used only at home. But Brian might become more hyperactive, more difficult to handle. I thanked him.

Now was the time to find out—while there were just the two of us, before another child arrived. I discontinued the midday dose, and the only change was that Brian's morning alertness continued into the afternoon. He still flapped and circled when danger seemed imminent—morning and afternoon.

Reading was designated dangerous; so was speaking. The sight of a book or a direct question produced prodigious fluttering.

Brian did not talk. He had not spoken at all since he was a toddler—or so his mother said. He had taught himself to read, and she claimed he had at one time read the newspaper out loud. Now when his father urged and urged him to read, he would run and hide his head in his mother's lap.

That first day he had screamed those few words—

"Gonna go to the doctor's"—and in his three weeks at school he had not spoken again. But the terrified, strangled "Awwwkk, awwwwkk" was diminishing, and in its place was some kind of jabber: "Obbety-dijeseomiwag, iwagotaplaggoblesetofo." This was said with normal inflection, but no matter how hard I strained there was no single word that I could understand. Our conversations were unintelligible, but happiness was growing.

I was gradually filling our bookcase with books from home. There had been none the first day; the Director had not provided any and I had not known what kind would be appropriate. My own children had loved a small book called *Read Me a Story*, and at the end of the first week I brought it to school.

During the morning I sat at our table with Brian and opened the book. He was immediately up and away, flapping.

I closed the book. "What? You do not like books either? You are so silly. All the best things in the world—and you decide you do not like them. I will read to myself then."

"Ogoahearetoyosf," from the corner of the room.

"All right. Fine. You stay there; I'll read here."

I picked a story at random and read aloud. About a car. A broken-down car that the family wanted to get rid of so they could buy a newer, fancier one. But in the end the old car shows its stuff and triumphs over the newer model.

And here comes Brian. Closer all the time. From the corner of the room to the middle to stand at the edge of the table. I start another story.

He is not afraid of the book; he is not afraid of my reading. Ahhh, it's just that he did not want to read himself—he was afraid that I would force him to read out loud to me from the book. Perhaps he has previously been urged too much, too often.

"Sit down," I say, "I'll read some more." He teeters on the brink, wanting to—not wanting to. "Not you, Bri. Me. It's my book. I'll do the reading."

This continues for four mornings. I begin to try to edge the book toward him; he will have none of it. Up and away, fluttering to the windowsill, to the shelf Dan has fixed up for us which holds our puzzles. Brian does these easily now, his hands quick and sure, calling to me as he finishes.

"Oolansethuzialfis."

"Good, Bri," I say and we leave the puzzle complete all day so that Dan can see it before he goes home.

"A beauty," he tells us, and Brian and I exchange looks of satisfaction.

Ah, now. That's what I will do. I will make a puzzle out of words. I copy the first page of the story about the car, which is Brian's favorite, onto a large piece of oaktag and then carefully I cut it into pieces. How many now? Careful. Not too easy. Not so easy that it will be obvious; not so difficult as to be discouraging. I snip with my scissors. Fifteen pieces. I put them in an old shoe box on the shelf beside the puzzles.

Brian finds them immediately. He hangs his coat upon his hook, comes close to me, "Maglateeu," he says, and I answer, "Good morning, Brian. I'm happy to see you."

Almost he smiles. He has not smiled yet. But this is close and I hug him without reservation.

I go back to mixing paints at the table and he runs his fingers over the shoe box. Something new. Suspicious. He flutters around the room once. Back to the box . . . he moves his fingers cautiously around its outside—he glances at me—I am absorbed in mixing paints.

He dips his fingers into the shoe box and feels the

pieces. Only pieces. Nothing to worry about. He lifts down the box and takes it to the puzzle board and spills the pieces of cardboard out and pushes them tentatively with his finger. Now he lines them up; he makes the top border even. Does he see that his pieces have made a sentence? Ahh, there's a flutter. Just a small one, just enough to show excitement. He knows; he's got it. The rest of the pieces fall quickly into place. And he turns to me. "Ha," he says. And I laugh.

"You are so smart," I say, "I cannot fool you at all. Right? You have made the first page of our story." I take the book from the bookshelf. "See. Here. The same words."

He holds the book, forgetting to be frightened. He holds the book—and when he turns the first page, I leave him. He does not need me now. He is reading by himself.

Chapter *TEN*

Matthew arrives unannounced. Brian and I are doing a picture puzzle of the United States; he is getting much better at it than I am; geography itself a puzzle to me.

"Hey," I say, "I'm the teacher. You're not supposed to be better than me." Grammar is another puzzle.

"Ha," he answers. Smiles come several times a day now.

The door bursts open. And there is the Director hanging on to the shoulder of a small blond boy.

"Whoop-de-doo," she says, "Slow down now. Whoa. Slow down. This is Matthew, Mary. Your new boy. Matthew Polatoff."

Matthew wrenches free. Kicks the Director in the ankle, eyes me, aims a kick in my direction—but my reflexes remain intact from Chris's training and he misses. This makes him even angrier, and he grabs at a corner of our small white bookcase and pushes it hard enough to dump it over and spill the books upon the floor.

"Hope you had your vitamins this morning, Mary," the Director calls cheerily as she backs out the door.

Brian is jumping up and down in the center of the room, awk-awking and flapping his arms.

Damn it, I think. Why does she have to dump him in here like this? I could have met him in the office ... stop it. Forget it. He's here.

"Hello, Matt," I say.

He rushes at me kicking, his small, handsome face contorted with anger, and I hold him at arm's length.

"You're in school now," I say. "You don't kick here."

But he's not about to stop. He kicks first with the right foot, then with the left; and some detached part of me notes that they seem to be equally preferred. What about his hands? Right- or left-handed? Is there a mixed dominance? I must read more tonight.

I try to wait him out; he is only six, after all—I have thirty more years than he does. I can hold him at bay indefinitely.

He also seems to be able to kick indefinitely, right foot, left foot. I do not wish to spend the entire morning like this, with Brian awk-awking while Matthew and I are locked in a strange embrace, slowly, weirdly picking up our feet and laying them down as in some tribal dance.

I let him go. He almost stumbles from the unexpected freedom—then recovers and takes his bearings. He sights Brian, a new target, and lunges toward him. Brian stands totally still, defenseless, and Matthew cracks his foot into Brian's ankle. Brian collapses to the floor, whimpering. And I grab Matthew. Put my foot behind his legs, bend his arm behind his back and bring him to the floor. Then I straddle his legs, facing his feet, and take off his shoes. He will not be able to do much damage in his stocking feet.

But now his dignity is outraged. He screams at me wordlessly and then bursts into tears. He goes to the far corner of the room, sits down on the floor, wraps his arms tightly around himself and rocks back and forth in misery. I go over and inspect Brian's leg; there is a bruise along the skin, but the bone is smooth under my fingers and there seems to be no real damage.

"You're okay," I tell him. "What happened anyway? What did you let him do that for?" Brian does not need sympathy; he needs to learn to fight.

"Iwanahomhehimel."

"Forget it," I say. "You're bigger than he is. Don't let him pick on you."

So now there were three of us. I made another label, MATTHEW, for the third coat hook.

The battles of the first day continued. Matthew spent most of his time in school in socks. I often wondered what his mother thought of the dirty black soles on his expensive socks, but she never mentioned it.

Matthew was an exquisitely dressed child. Everything was coordinated, expensive, cleaned and pressed. His mother was a former model and now his three-year-old brother, blond and beautiful, was modeling too. Each day when Matthew arrived, his clothes looked, not merely clean, but brand new. Each day when he left they were dirty and tear-stained.

And so were mine. Matthew was too much for me; slowly he was wearing me down. Each day I was more tired; each day he fought harder.

He was a handsome boy. Thick, wheat-colored hair; a broad, deep forehead, wide-set dark blue eyes. His features were straight, regular, he looked like an illustration from a Christmas catalog. Only a small strawberry birthmark on his neck marred the picture of perfection, and when he became angry the area surrounding the mark also turned a deep dull red.

Matthew was angry most of the time; there was more rage inside him than I had ever seen in anyone.

There was no eating or toilet problem. He wolfed his food, used the toilet regularly, then scrubbed his hands and face to get them clean, cleaner, until the fair, sensitive skin was red, almost raw. He had virtually no speech, but his hearing seeemed to be intact. He could hear my watch tick when I held it behind his head, and if I whispered to him with my head turned away he still understood what I was saying. He could make the beginning, elementary sounds, but was unable to form an *s*, *l*, or *w* or the stop plosives, *t* and *d*. He tried hard to speak; in fact, the only time I had his total attention was when we worked on sounds and letters, and then he would rivet his dark eyes on mine almost as if he could draw the words out of me and into himself.

I would sit at the low table opposite Brian and Matt, and while Brian completed the United States puzzle—eyeing us warily but continuing his work, making a map now, tracing each wooden state—I would work with Matt.

He would reach across the table.

"*M, M*"—his voice urgent.

"What, Matt? What is it?"

And he would grab for the large cardboard letters in my hand and find the M. I had cut the letters from sandpaper and pasted them on the cardboard squares, thinking perhaps the touch would help him. (It was not until much later that I learned to call this tactile, kinesthetic teaching; and later still that I learned I should not have used letters but actual objects that had meaning for him.) But Matthew would trace the M with his finger, as I had shown him, and say, "Mm, Mm, Mm." Then he would reach for my hand, if I did not do it soon enough, and put my fingers against his mouth and repeat, "Mm, Mm." Then I would replace my fingers with his own and he would say again, "Mm, Mm, Mm," feeling the vibration with his fingertips.

But if I turned from him for a minute—only a minute—to help Brian trace the jagged edges of Pennsylvania, he would be filled with fury; grab the puzzles and throw them to the floor. If I tried to read a story to both of them at once he would start a buzzing noise between his teeth and in his throat, gradually increasing the volume until my voice could not be heard. Filled with frustration, I would lay down the book and look at him, and he would laugh at his victory.

Dan came into my room one morning as I was sitting on Matthew's legs, removing his shoes after an early assault.

"Want some help?" he asked.

Perhaps if anyone else had asked, I would have been too proud to admit my weariness, my sense of failure, but to Dan I said only, "I'd love it."

"We're going over to the duck pond now to feed the ducks. Want to come?"

It was the first of many trips we made together. Dan loved to take his class outside, teaching them to run, throw, catch, hammer together an outside run for the gerbils they had in their room. He teased me about my "academics"—the alphabet, numbers, my exercises with body image: "Feel your head, touch it—like this, see ... your neck, feel that and your shoulders—there. Good. See how they fit into each other—now your arms." And so it would go until we reached the feet.

Dan teased me, but he came to my room one morning before school started and said, "How about a swap today?"

"What do you mean? What kind?"

"Suppose you take Stuart for the morning and I'll take Matt. Stuart is a funny kid, you know. Nobody can get close to him. He's smart as hell—I'm sure of it—but he's also smart enough to play dumb. And he knows just what to do to turn people off. Instinctively, he seems to figure out what will bug a person most and then do it. With me, for instance, he acts like a goddamn fairy—kissing my hand, telling me how sweet I am."

Dan was big and rugged-looking with broad shoulders, strong forearms. His hair was always tousled and his clothes clean but rumpled. For the first time I wondered who did his laundry; he obviously played the field, a different girl each week waiting for him in the parking lot after school. None of us discussed our lives away from school. The only exception was our own children. All of us, except Dan and the Director, had children at home, and occasionally they would call and leave messages with Zoe or be sick and need care at home. So we got brief glimpses of each other's outside lives through our children; but other than that there was no talk of our personal lives, mostly, I suppose, because there was no time. We were always with the children. In this school there was no teacher's room, no coffee break, not even a lunch hour. As teachers we talked to each other in snatches, and usually it was something urgently concerning one of the children at school.

"So," Dan continued, "my idea is that I'll take Matt off your hands, take him outside with us, and run the pants off him. So by the time I bring him back he'll be so tired he won't be able to raise a foot, much less kick you."

"And in return I'll take Stuart—and save you from homosexual attack? What if I don't want my hand kissed either?"

"You'll do all right. Besides, he'll figure out something else for you."

"All right. Except if he really is faggy, he probably needs to be with you—know that you're his friend. How about if I keep Stuart for an hour, work with him and Brian, and then we all come join you outside?"

Dan considered. "Okay. That will be even better. I'll bring Stuart in after Circle. You get in some of the letter-sound stuff with Matt before we get here, though why Francis, our esteemed speech pathologist, can't help you with that, I don't know. Incidentally, did you know that's what he is now, that's what he calls himself—a speech pathologist instead of speech therapist."

"Why? Is there a difference?"

"God knows. Listen, I've got to get back now. I'll come by right after Circle."

"Okay, good. I'll have Matt ready. By the way, what's the Director going to say about this?"

"She's not even going to know unless you tell her."

"Oh Dan, I'm not sure that's right."

"Mary, my God. You're such an innocent. Cool it now, all right?"

"All right." I was not really worried. Dan talked tough, but he was really very gentle. I had watched him wash skinned knees and bandage them. I had watched him hold the gerbils while the boys cleaned their cage. He was gentle and I trusted him.

He left and then stuck his head back in the door.

"I won't have time to talk once the kids come. I wanted to tell you where we'll be. Across the street."

"In the graveyard?" I asked in amazement.

"Yeah, great place. Lots of room for baseball, and when the kids get tired of that they can climb Parsons' mausoleum. How's your baseball?"

"Not very good. I throw underhand."

"Oh, my God." Dan moans in mock horror. "Underhand. Wouldn't you know? Junior throws underhand."

To say that Stuart Wagner was a strange kid was an understatement. He was ten; a skinny, gangling kid with red hair and steel-rimmed glasses.

When Dan brought him in and took Matt out, Stuart merely stood looking at me mildly. Finally he said, "Aren't you the darling teacher, though. For your age." And then he stuck his hand down the back of his trousers inside his belt and massaged his buttocks.

I decided I was not going to endure what I didn't like.

"Take your hand out of your pants, Stuart."

Stuart complied but won the round, removing his hand slowly and then smelling his finger with great concentration.

"Okay," I said, "let's get started."

I arranged the alphabet cards on the chalk tray of the blackboard and started the morning drill. Dan had told me he wasn't sure how much Stuart knew. Some days he seemed to be able to remember the alphabet and count to one hundred; other days he knew nothing. By the end of that first hour I was sure Stuart knew the entire alphabet and a lot more, but wasn't going to let anybody find it out.

I'd say, "All right, Stuart, let's read off these letters. I'll start. A, B . . ."

Stuart's voice joined mine: "C, D, E, Fuck . . ."

"That's F," I said.

"Oh. I thought it stood for 'fuck.' "

"F's a letter—'fuck' is a word. I want the letter."

"Oh. Fine. F, G, H . . ."

I loved the kid. Funny, awkward, provocative, trying to disrupt me, make me lose my composure. Swearing was not the way to do it; swearing had never had much meaning for me, "duck" was almost the same as "fuck." I really couldn't see why people got so upset about it. Besides, the person I knew who swore the most was Helga. And I loved Helga.

It turned out to be a good arrangement, swapping Stuart and Matt. It was true, Matt came back tired and happy. Dan liked him and treated him in a way that was both rough and gentle. He would run with him, tackle him, roll on the ground wrestling with him, letting Matt win occasionally so that he could sit in triumph upon Dan's chest. Dan also smacked him—something I could never do. One day we stopped at the A & P to buy bread for the ducks, and Matt deliberately knocked six jars of baby food to the floor. Dan picked him up, held him under one arm, and smacked him across his bottom.

But he also held him gently. Once Matt fell off the bike that Dan was teaching him to ride and scraped his arm, and Dan carried him to my room. When I came back with water and first-aid cream, I could hear him saying, "Okay, bear. Easy now. We'll get that fixed in a minute." And Matt sat quietly within Dan's arms while I washed and bandaged the scrape.

The swap was good for Brian too. Stuart was exceedingly verbal and Brian was fascinated by him, particularly his rudeness to me. Rebellion in another form. And sometimes he got away with it. I consoled myself that my lost rounds with Stuart were good for Brian. I wanted him to see that speech was effective. Not very good for classroom discipline, but then I was not much concerned with formal discipline just then. In any event, Brian was making more and more sounds and noises; it is true there was a weird falsetto Donald Duck quality about them, but the output was increasing and Brian hovered closer and closer as I worked with Matt.

Each morning I worked with Matthew's speech. We were exempt from Circle those early weeks, the Director saying it would be too much for my new boys at first, and so during that forty-five-minute period Matthew and I would sit together at the table.

I had no right to work on speech problems, and I knew it. I had had no training in this specialized field. True, I had had no training in any field except my psychology courses at Wellesley. Somehow, though, speech therapy seemed to me more specific, more difficult than teaching a child to eat or go to the bathroom or read.

Each week I would ask Francis if he couldn't take some time to work with Matthew. And each week he answered: "He has a language problem, not a speech problem. When he becomes a happy child this will cure itself."

No, I would think, that's not true. With Brian, yes. There is some puzzle there—delicate, intricate. I would not let you near Brian at this stage. But with Matt it's different; there is some mechanical problem. I know, I watch him, I see him try so hard. He wants to speak, but he cannot form the letters.

Out loud I say, "He has difficulty forming some of

the sounds. For instance, even when he wants to he cannot seem to make the *t* sound—you know, like in 'toe.' If you could just show him how to do it, I think it would mean a lot to him."

"He is not ready for that. We must wait for him to be ready."

"Could you just show me, then, so I could show him?"

Francis' voice grows strident, he forgets his well-modulated tones; obviously I have gone too far. "I repeat, the child is not ready. Your job is to help him to find happiness within himself. You must not be so impatient, Mary—or attempt to blame someone else if you cannot do your job."

But I wasn't blaming you. I just wanted to help. I know so little—you have all that training that I don't have. And I know, I really know, that instead of just waiting for Matt to become happy, we should give him a chance to learn. It would help him to be happy if he could learn to make the *t* sound. Let him have the chance—he needs to feel he's learning, doing something about his problem.

Out loud I say nothing. I decide that he is right about one thing: I must learn to be more patient. I will practice with you, Francis; you have so much time. I smile at him and say softly, "Maybe you're right. I'll talk to you again when you come next week."

"Fine, Mary. That's a much better attitude."

Francis may have lots of time, but Matthew doesn't, and before I go home I drive into the city and buy a manual on speech therapy, a tape recorder, and a mirror. And every morning while the rest of the school goes to Circle I get the mirror and tape recorder from the closet and set them on the table in front of me. Matthew races to the chair beside me and we begin the exercises in the manual, with variations. He blows out the candles on the birthday cake I make him out of clay. More candles each day. Brian is fascinated and cannot stay away. He hovers, watching me build the cake. "How old are you today, Matt? Let's see. You were five last week, how about being six today?" And then seven, eight, finally up to nine. "You're big today, Matt. Nine. Nine candles. Do you think you can blow them all out?"

Brian leaves his puzzles and flutters over. "Ucanahanicusisonesx."

"Okay, Bri," I say, "join us." And I build a clay cake for him too.

As we do more exercises it becomes apparent that Matt cannot lift his tongue. He can move it from side to side and point it downward, but he has difficulty raising it.

He watches in the mirror as my tongue goes out and up, aiming for my nose.

"Pretend we just had ice cream with our cake," I say, "strawberry ice cream"—knowing his favorite— "and we have it all over our mouths, our lips. Lick it off. Way up there—you've still got some on your upper lip. Good, Matt. That's it." And his tongue did touch his upper lip.

"Minosicntuchminowfmitng," says Brian as he licks away with his long tongue.

After school that afternoon I played the tape back listening to Matt's noises, planning the set of exercises for the next day. It seemed to me that his *t* sound was getting clearer. I read the book: the tongue is on the gum ridge behind the front upper teeth; I practiced it myself. True, that's where it was.

I slow the speed of the tape to hear Matt more

clearly. Suddenly I hear a voice saying, "My nose. I can touch my nose with my tongue."

I can't believe it. I play it over and over. It is Brian—Brian speaking in full sentences. I go back and replay the whole tape at the slower speed.

There's his voice again: "You cannot have nine candles. He is only six."

Over and over I play the tape while tears slide down my face. I forget the time and when Dan opens the door he says, "I thought I heard voices. What's going on? You all right, Mair? Why are you sitting here with no lights?"

"Listen," I say. And I play the tape again.

"I don't get it. Who's that? Why are you listening to some kid talk about candles? Come on. Tell me. What is it? What's wrong?"

"Listen," I say, "Dan, listen."

I want him to hear it. I want so much for it to be real, not some dream of mine. I can't have just imagined it, can I?

I play the tape again. It is so clear to me now. Brian had never stopped speaking—he had simply revved up his speech so that it made no sense. He had taught himself to talk in the souped-up high voice of a 45 record player at 78 speed—but on the slowed-down tape recorder you can hear his actual speech. Instead of weird gobbledygook, you hear the words.

Dan is leaning forward, listening intently. "Play it again, Mary. Shhh. Oh my God, it's Brian. Right? That's Bri . . . talking. He said, 'I can touch my nose with my tongue.'"

He'd heard it. Dan had heard it too. It was not just in my head. I put my head down on the table—I cannot help it. I do not want to cry but I cannot help it. And the tape recorder plays again.

I can hear my voice, slowed by the tape, saying,

"Good, Matt. That's it," and Brian's voice: "My nose, I can touch my nose with my tongue."

And Dan's own voice saying above the tape recorder, "There, Junior, don't cry. It's good. It's fine."

Chapter *ELEVEN*

Time was going too fast. Memorial Day weekend was coming up, which meant that there were only three more weeks of school left. Not enough time, the Director said, to bring in another child. So we continued as we were—Brian, Matthew, and myself in the converted storeroom, with Stuart trading places with Matt after Circle and then all of us going outside to join Dan and his class of older boys. Tom, stolid and deliberate, no longer running wildly, hand across his eyes, but still retreating into the turtleneck of his sweater when danger was imminent; Ivan, the most beautiful of the children, with red curly hair and the grace of a Russian dancer, reminding me always of Stravinsky and whirling music as he leaped and jumped; and Jeffy Olivero, wan and thin, walking curved like a question mark with one hand raised above his head, thumb and forefinger pinched together—his favorite position, Dan told me, because he slept that way each night with his widowed mother, holding her earlobe between his thumb and forefinger.

"Why?" I asked. "Why does she allow it?"

"It's not a question of allowing it—she loves it," Dan said.

Sometimes now when we came in from our baseball games in the graveyard we ate together in Dan's room—his four boys and my two. Zoe was a fan of Dan's and she loved bringing lunch to his room—

"the Diner's Club" she called it—and cheerfully she pushed the hot cart down to us, coming back later to bring us coffee and sit and talk with Dan and me for a moment before she went back to the office.

The boys played quietly around us as we drank our coffee, Ivan and Tom building with erector sets or simply spinning the pieces around and around, Matthew rocking wordlessly beside the record player, Brian and Stuart at the blackboard reconstructing one of the prizewinning games on television. They were both TV devotees and would play endlessly, drawing prizes on the blackboard—washing machines, TV sets, mink coats. They took turns being the emcee; rather we made them take turns; they both fought for the position and the chance to say, "And now for the big question, the chance to win a brand-new Whirlpool washer-dryer with super-speed extractors. Are you ready? The question is: How many miles from the earth to the moon?" Or, "Who is currently in power in Chile?" They parroted the questions, rarely knowing the answers, which didn't seem to bother them at all; at least they didn't have to draw more prizes. Only if you won was the prize erased.

It was great for Brian's speech; I could say to him, "Slow it down, Bri, the contestant cannot understand the question." And he would repeat what he had said slowly and distinctly. I had played the tape for him a few days after my discovery of his speech. I had thought about it for a long time and finally decided there was no better way to tell him what I knew.

Brian loved the tape recorder and eagerly settled himself to listen, giggling as he listened to me urge Matthew to lick his lip. The second time I played the tape, I slowed the speed so that my voice came out low and draggy.

Brian was immediately up flapping.

Did he know what was coming?

I couldn't tell; there were only the fluttering and flapping beside me.

"It's okay, Bri. Listen. Listen to where we're both talking."

He stays still, still beside me. And his voice comes out of the record player: "My nose, I can touch my nose with my tongue."

Quickly, before he can move, I turn off the tape.

"You're so tricky," I say. "Can you still do it fast?"

No threat in doing it fast, I hoped—and yet we could acknowledge what he'd done.

"Minosicntuchminowfmitng"—the same high falsetto.

"Okay," I say. "Now when I turn the knob one-quarter of a degree to the left, I want to hear it a little bit slower." I turn the middle button on his shirt and he looks at me with solemn eyes.

"I can touch my nose with my tongue," he says.

"Now a little bit faster, Bri."

He speeds the tempo. "Icantouchmynosewithmy-tongue."

"How about louder?"

"I CAN TOUCH MY NOSE WITH MY TONGUE."

"Softer?"

A bare whisper: "I can touch my nose with my tongue."

"Can you change the tape?" It is a big question and I ask it softly. He has played with the one sentence, been willing to manipulate it, to acknowledge to me that he can control the way it is produced. If now he will do it with another set of words, I think he will be okay.

Brian sits on the desk looking at me solemnly, not speaking but no longer fluttering.

Suddenly he says, "Mary say it."

"Me? You want me to do it?" His own words as he speaks are clear. I can hardly contain the excitement I feel, but I try not to let it interfere.

Brian's hand reaches toward the button on my blouse.

"Say it," he says again.

"I can touch my nose . . ." I say.

Brian turns my button, my invisible control, to the right.

"Faster. Do it faster."

"Icantouchmynosewithmytongue."

"No," he says, "Like this." And once more he mouths the weird, falsetto gobbledygook. I try again—but he is far better at it than me.

He giggles and says, "Play it again."

That was all there was. No big speeches or even planned lessons. All I did with Bri was remind him to slow down when excitement raced his words. Pronouns remained a problem at times. Brian trusted them not at all. "You" was confusing—sometimes it meant one person, sometimes another. He was not yet sure enough of his own self to trust it to a pronoun, and so he often referred to himself as Brian and me as Mary.

However, he was so delighted with his new power of communication that he talked all the time, fluttering with excitement, giggling at his jokes, which he also collected from TV programs and delivered to us at school. His memory was amazing; he knew the names of each state and its capital and could recite them at will. It was obvious that I was going to have to develop a structured academic program for him; he should have the chance to progress through the steps of math and reading and science . . .

"What do you say we climb the mountain on Friday?" Dan's voice interrupted my thoughts.

"What mountain?"

"At Milbury. It's a state park, about twelve hundred acres. The Boy Scouts have campgrounds there for overnights. It has a lake, good wide paths, and a small-to-medium mountain. We could walk up in the morning, have lunch, then come back in the afternoon."

I was doubtful. "That's an awful lot of walking, Dan."

"Aw, Mary, come on now. That's what you said when we went to the lake. You said it would be too much for the boys. Remember?"

He was right. I had thought that the trip we had gone on two weeks before was going to be too difficult. We had walked four miles around a lake on a narrow path, hiking single file, the six boys between us—Dan going first, breaking off branches that grew across the trail, calling to warn us of rocks and holes. I brought up the rear, carrying discarded sweaters as the day grew warmer and the boys hotter.

But they had loved it. No one had ever done this kind of thing with these children before. The Director in her fund-raising speeches often referred to them as "attic children," meaning that many of the parents had kept the children secluded at home, never taking them out, hiding them, unable to cope with them in the outside world.

But Dan took them out, opening the world to them, expecting them to be able to cope with it. And they did. They adored him and followed where he led. In the following, their legs and backs got stronger—they grew. I followed, too—I had met another master teacher.

So on the Friday morning before Memorial Day we all gathered in Dan's room. The day was bright and beautiful, the sun hot in the clear blue sky. The boys had brought their notes of permission and their sandwiches wrapped in wax paper.

We had gone shopping the day before and had bought marshmallows and Band-Aids, and Dan packed these along with the sandwiches into a brown shoulder pack. He had also brought two canteens and a camera. Tom and Ivan were to carry the canteens, Dan the shoulder pack; the camera was entrusted to me.

We were all in blue jeans and sneakers except Matthew. He was dressed in gold-green Bermuda shorts with olive green socks and matching shirt; as usual, everything looked brand-new and beautiful, and he was extraordinarily handsome with his blond hair contrasting with the dull green shirt. I was concerned about his bare legs—the rest of us had the protection of jeans—and I went to ask Zoe for an extra pair of long pants, but there was no extra clothing (except diapers for Louis in Joyce's room—how long ago that seemed). When I returned to Dan's room the boys and he were gone. A note on the blackboard said, *We'll meet you in the parking lot.*

Dan and I rode up front in his Volkswagen bus, and the six boys in back. They were used to riding together; Friday trips had become a regular thing and everyone had his favorite seat. We talked a little, sang a few songs, but for the most part we were quiet—all of us were excited about climbing a mountain. Dan had already hiked this particular mountain and he had drawn a picture of it on the blackboard for us, showing the parking lot where we would leave the car, the wide trail weaving up the mountain, a lake at one far end, even a small brook. I was as eager as the boys: I had never climbed a mountain either.

We pulled into the camping ground parking lot about ten o'clock. It was deserted except for us. Dan showed us the pump on the west side beyond the picnic tables, and each of us had a drink from the tin dipper. I was pleased with the pump. It took two to get a drink and was a natural lesson in cooperation. Someone had to hold the dipper; someone had to pump the handle. The boys had never seen this form of producing water before and would have lingered for hours pumping and drinking. Progress has its minuses: you can turn a faucet alone.

At last we were ready, canteens filled, pack in place on Dan's shoulders, and he said, "All right, troops, let's go."

The boys bounded off ahead of us and Dan let them go, quickening his own walk to stay close to them. I walked behind them, examining the trees, delighting in the moss, the rocks, the small scurryings just off the path.

We walked for perhaps half an hour before we reached the brook, larger than I had thought it would be, about fifteen feet across; fast-moving water. The children ranged along the edge, watching intently as the water pushed over the rocky streambed, tumbling by us. There was no bridge, and I waited for Dan to point out the detour we would take around it. Instead, he said, "I'll cross first and test the stones, then come back and we'll all go over together."

I could not believe it. Did he really think the children could walk across that wild water—the brook filled with the recently melted snows of winter? I moved close to him and spoke in a low voice. "Dan, they can't cross here. It's too dangerous."

A steady look from Dan, his blue eyes even bluer with sky and water so close to him, his own voice as low as mine. "If I had thought it was too dangerous, I wouldn't have brought them. Trust me, Mary."

Dan walked across the brook slowly, testing each stone for steadiness. Once he bent and brushed some leaves from one of the rocks.

When he came back to us he said, "I'll go over first with Matt; the rest of you wait here with Mary. Then I want you to walk across one at a time. Wait until the person in front of you reaches the other bank and then start. The rocks are good and steady. You won't have any trouble."

Dan went first—step ... wait ... look toward Matt ... smile. Matt followed, watching Dan closely, putting his feet in exactly the same place Dan had. When they reached the other side we sent up a small spontaneous cheer—"Ya-aay!"

Matt tried to cheer back, but couldn't and so he clapped instead. Happy, filled with pride.

"Okay, Tom, come on. You're next," Dan called.

Tom hesitated, ducked inside his turtleneck, then emerged, and with unerring accuracy and incredible speed raced across the rocks, only his arm across his eyes betraying the fear he felt. We cheered him, too, and Dan put his arm around Tom's shoulders, "Good boy, Tom. What a tiger."

Then Jeffy mincing across, arm still upraised, gently pinching the unseen earlobe as though his mother would lead him across. Ivan danced over.

Then Stuart, rubbing his thick glasses as he waited his turn, at the last minute turning back saying, "After you, Mary. Ladies first."

I shook my head. Brian was fluttering behind me and Dan called, "Move it, Stuart. Move your butt across that brook. Fast."

Only Brian left now. And me. But Brian was getting more and more nervous, his speech was too fast to be intelligible. He made one false start and splashed water on the side of his shoe. "Awk-awk"— back to my side.

"Come on, Mair." Dan called. "Get the rest of your class over here. It's getting late."

"Bri," I said, "I'll go first. You come right behind me."

I started off. The water made more noise than I'd realized. One step, wait, look back, smile—just as Dan had done. But when I looked back, Brian was still on the bank. I couldn't leave him there, but if I went back he'd never come. Dan roared something from the other side, I stood on the first rock, waiting, listening to myself. Hey, what now?

Ahhh, finally. "Okay, Bri," I called. "Are you ready? Now for the big sixty-four-thousand-dollar question. For the chance to win a brand-new Impala Chevrolet with bucket seats, air conditioning, and tape deck—can you tell me how many rocks there are in this path to the other side?"

Brian laughed. He joined me on the first rock.

"One," he said. He moved past me to the next stone. "Two." I nodded. He went one more. "Three." And now I followed him. "Nineteen, twenty, twenty-one, twenty-two, twenty-three. There are twenty-three rocks, Mary."

"Good for you, Brian. You win the Chevy Impala."

"Bucket seats," he giggled. "Say with bucket seats."

"With bucket seats and air conditioning," I said.

Dan reached and helped him up the bank and then me. I hugged Bri. We had all made it. We were very proud of ourselves.

It was pleasant walking now. Dan set a moderate pace and we all fell into it, moving in an easy rhythm. I glanced at my watch: eleven o'clock.

By eleven-thirty it was no longer so pleasant. The trail was steep now. Jeffy had stumbled twice; we were all breathing hard.

"How much farther?" I called to Dan. He waved us to a stop. Brian, Jeffy and I sat down.

"We're almost there now. You're a fantastic bunch of climbers. Tom, how's the water? Let's all have a drink."

We passed the canteen around. I had never drunk from one before; there was a metallic taste but the water seemed incredibly sweet.

"Okay. Let's go," Dan said. "This is the hardest part. Don't try to go too fast. Stay in line up this part of the trail. Don't try to push past. Watch the man in front of you. Okay, let's go."

It was steep. All rock now. I wondered how the boys did it. Matt was as agile as a mountain goat, not even breathing hard, scrambling behind Dan.

Brian and I were last. In some places it was so steep that our hands touched the path as we climbed up, but there was an exhilaration: we were doing it.

And then suddenly we were there. We were at the top. The ground was level and the sky was pure blue above us and we lay there on our backs laughing and calling to each other.

Finally someone said, "I'm hungry," and we opened the knapsack and ate our sandwiches, Brian his saltines. I said to Dan, "I'm happy," and he grinned back at me.

After lunch we lay down and rested before our walk back. The sun was warm and I think I dozed a little.

Suddenly something was wrong. I sat up, frightened. What was it? Everything was still beautiful, no clouds; the others were still resting, lying down. Dan was leaning against a large boulder whittling.

I counted heads. Five. There should be six. Ahhh. The blond one. Where was Matthew? I moved over to sit by Dan.

"Where's Matt?" I asked.

"Over there, by the big rock."

"Where?"

"Well, he was there just a second ago."

Dan walked to the large rock, perhaps a dozen feet away. Then farther. Then back to me. "I can't see him. I'll walk out a bit. Be right back."

He was gone fifteen minutes.

When he came back his face was grave. "There's no sign of him. We'd better organize ourselves."

I was frightened. Matt was so little, only six; but worse than that, he had no speech. If he had been hurt or was lost, he could not call to us. I called, "Matt? Matthew? Where are you? Clap your hands, Matt!"

The other five children were awake now, alert, standing close to us. We all listened intently but there was no response. Suddenly there was a cracking noise down the mountain; Dan ran to peer in that direction, but before he had gone three feet all was silent again.

"Listen, Mary, can you keep the boys here? I can go faster without them; I'll cover as much territory as I can. You keep the others with you and keep calling to Matt from time to time. He may have just wandered a short way and your voice will help direct him back here."

"Dan, how could I have let him get lost? It never occurred to me that he would leave us. Everyone was tired and so happy. I should have kept him beside me. Oh Dan, he can't even call us."

"It's nobody's fault. Or if it's anybody's, it's mine. I was the one who was keeping watch. I knew you were resting . . . you looked so tired. Anyway, there's no time to talk now. I'll find him. Don't worry. You just hold the fort here. Do you think you can manage my boys?"

"Yes," I said. But I was not sure at all. Tom and Jeffy were both almost as tall as I was.

"Good." He looked at his watch. "Ten to one. I'll be back by one-thirty."

He left, walking rapidly, then came back and unbuckled his belt and took off his knife. "Here. Keep this. Use it if you need to."

I stood holding the knife in its leather case. Why had he given it to me? Were there animals? Snakes? He couldn't have meant the children.

We watched him go, Tom calling, "Dan, Dan, can I come?" And Dan calling back over his shoulder, "No, Tom. Wait there. I won't be long."

"I won't be long," echoed Tom.

I was near tears. Guilty, frightened. Ashamed. What would the Director say? She had trusted me. What about Matt's mother? And his clothes—his stupid clothes—the same color as the leaves. How could Dan ever find him?

Still, I was a teacher. Dan had left me with his class, and I must not now lose these as well. And they could easily leave me, go running after Dan— fall—be lost in all directions.

"Let's make a circle," I said. I sat down and Brian sat on one side of me, Stuart on the other. Tom pulled his turtleneck over his entire head. Ivan and Jeffy did not move.

"We must help Matt find his way back to us." There was no point in pretending. Matt obviously wasn't there. "We'll take turns calling to him." I wanted Tom to join us. I felt that if he would come and sit down, the others would too. I slipped my watch off my wrist and held it out to Tom.

"Tom, you be the timekeeper. Every five minutes we'll call Matt. We'll try to keep calling as long as we can—a whole minute or two." I didn't know if Tom could tell time. "Every time the big hand points to a number, you tell us, Tom, and we'll call."

"That's a darling watch," Stuart said.

"Shut up, Stuart!" Tom shouted, suddenly pushing the turtleneck back inside his jacket. He sat down opposite me and reached for the watch.

"It is one-o-one. Call the one o'clock call," said Tom.

"Matthew! Matt!" I yelled in relief.

Their voices joined mine. "Matthew! Matt! We're over here, Matt. Come on over here."

We stopped, listening. Nothing. Not even Dan. But he wouldn't call back; that would be confusing to Matt, upsetting to the others.

"It is one-o-five. Call," said Tom, and again we yelled Matt's name, stopping sooner this time. It was hard to keep calling when there was no answer, only a vague, distant echo.

"It's one-o-five and a half. Call," said Stuart, mimicking Tom.

"And a half. Goddamn fucking son of a bitch," said Tom as he hit Stuart.

"Cut it out!" I said, getting between them, trying to sound authoritarian. "Cut it out now." I had better think of something, get them interested, diverted, keep them from fighting.

"Listen," I said, "we can't just keep shouting his name. That won't do any good. What we need to do is think up something that will make him want to come back."

"Tell him we got chocolate," said Stuart. "He likes chocolate."

"Tell Matt Mary isn't mad at him," said Brian, fluttering.

"It's one-ten. Call," said Tom.

We lasted somehow, calling, thinking up things that Matt liked, seeing who could call the loudest, the longest.

At exactly one-thirty Dan appeared—alone. "No luck," he said.

He sat down beside me. I handed him the knife and he turned it in his hands as he talked.

"How are we going to work this now? It took us an hour and a half to get up here. We have to get the kids back by three at the latest or the buses won't wait and everyone will go berserk. I've been thinking about what you said, about Matt being happy. You're right, he was—but maybe that's why he left us. He didn't want to go back; he likes it here. If that's true, he won't want us to find him— and in that case it could take a long, long time. It seems to me we should get the rest of the kids back. What do you think? Do you want to hike the five kids down and drive the car back? Or do you want to wait here alone? One of us should stay in case Matt does try to come back to us."

"Maybe he's gone to the car. Maybe he followed the trail back to the parking lot and is waiting for us there. He's smart. He could have done that," I say hopefully, but I am grasping at straws. And even as I say it I remember the trail. The brook. Full of white, rushing water and Matthew standing on the rocks . . . oh God, suppose he's already fallen in?

"You can go faster than I can. You go. But call Doris, or Zoe if she's not there. Tell them what's happened. Tell them we'll have to call the police or someone to help us hunt. Is there a phone anywhere?"

"Yes. There's one in a shelter just beyond the brook." Dan's eyes lock with mine, and we both know what the other is thinking. "I'll call," he says. "Okay, boys. We're going down. Get ready."

I stand up to wave to them. And Brian flutters around me, arms moving rapidly up and down. "Not going to leave Mary. Not on the mountain. No. No. Take Mary, Dan. Dan. Take Mary."

"I'll be down in a little, Bri. Now listen, you look hard for Matthew the whole way down. You've got good eyes and you know him best."

Dan says, "If I find him, I'll come back. I'll call the school and then I'll come and get you. I'll be back as fast as I can. If I don't find him, I'll still call the school and get help started—but I'll take the kids back before I come back for you." He puts the knife quietly in my hand.

"All right, Dan."

But Stuart stands stubbornly still.

"Hey, Tom," he says, "give Mary her watch. She needs her watch."

I stand watching them—the watch in one hand, the knife in the other—until they are out of sight.

I go and sit against the same boulder where Dan had leaned, whittling, not so long before. The sun is still bright and I am tempted to walk out and search among the rocks and underbrush, but I know how poor my sense of direction is and I decide against it. It would not help to have to search for me as well as for Matt. And so I sit and call to him as we did before, but the boys are gone now and my single voice seems lonely on the mountain, and the minutes seem to be moving so slowly. I stop looking at my watch and making the five-minute calls and just make up a song about a mountain and a boy—and sing the chorus as loudly as I can: "Matt, Matthew. Come back. I wait for you here."

By four-thirty I knew that Matt hadn't been waiting by the car. Dan would have been back for me by now if he had found him. Clouds had begun to move over the sky, and it was turning much cooler. I was not sure if this was the way evening arrived here or if it meant that rain was coming. I was cold, even in my jeans, and my heart ached as I thought of Matt in his gold Bermuda shorts. Where could he have gone? Was Dan right? Could it be that he didn't want to go back? That somehow he would rather stay here ... and remembering his too-perfect little brother, I decided that this was quite possible. Ahh, Mary, careful; perhaps it was only school to which he did not want to return.

Over and over I thought how I should not have come on this trip—or at least should have kept Matt beside me. I had not known him well enough to move away so soon; I did not have enough keys to him yet. Where would he have gone? He had loved climbing, even in his inappropriate clothes; why had I let him come in those clothes? I should have insisted on jeans and sneakers. But even so, he had done well, climbing at the head of the line of boys, never falling behind. He had eaten his sandwich, sitting next to Brian and me, and then two marshmallows. I remember giving him those. And water. I passed him the canteen. But then what? What had he done then? I had picked up the wax paper and Saran Wrap from the sandwiches and put it in the knapsack. Then I had sat down; everyone was quiet, resting; Brian and Stuart were using small stones to try and draw TV prizes on the rock. I think I remember Matt sitting near Dan, arms folded around himself, watching while Dan whittled.

I know I put the paper-filled knapsack under my head and stretched out on the sun-warmed rock. I remember the feeling of safety and of peace.

That must have been when it happened. Matt must have wandered off in those few minutes. I should not have lain down ... don't think about that now, that doesn't help. Think about lunch, Matt ... sandwiches, marshmallows, canteen, sitting arms folded. Why would he get up right then? What did he do after lunch at school? The bathroom. He always went to the bathroom after lunch at school to wash. He had been taught somewhere to be clean, too clean. That must be it. He must have felt hot and sticky from the climb, the marshmallows, and gone to look for a place to wash—and decided either to stay or else tried to come back and been unable to find his way. My heart sank as I remembered the only place he would know to look for water, and I groaned out loud. And yet there was the pump . . .

Loud noises. No voices, just rocks slipping; motion. Someone, something, was coming. Run. Should I run? But where would I run? I loosened the knife in its leather case and waited.

"Hallooo up there." Two heavy-booted men came up beside me. "We're looking for a six-year-old. Boy. Blond hair. Green clothes. Seen him?" The description reduced Matt to microscopic size, worse than an obituary. And yet, Dan must have called. He must have at least gotten down to the brook and not found Matt hurt or . . . We traded information, the troopers and I; they thought I should leave the mountain; it was five o'clock and the sky was darkening, lowering there on the mountain. But Dan had said he would be back and he would be tired and hungry by then, anxious to get home himself; I didn't want him to have to search for me. I stayed and the troopers left, leaving me their extra flashlight and assuring me that they would call my family from the next shelter.

I went back and leaned against the boulder again, sitting with my knees under my chin, arms wrapped around them to keep warm. I was conscious of being alone, the darkness like eternity around me. I had the feeling I should be thinking big thoughts, but all that filled my head were images of Matt, leaning toward me across our worktable, grabbing my hand, pressing my fingers against his lips, the small strawberry mark against the white skin on his neck, his dark blue eyes burning with urgency as he said, "Mm. Mm."

Darkness was complete now, a thick, black pool above me; there were no stars, only a lopsided moon beginning to rise against the eastern sky.

"Hallo up there. Hallooo. We've found him. Are you still there? Come down. Can you come down?"

I recognize the troopers' voices and shout back, "Coming. I'm coming. Is he all right?" I call as I start down the path, slipping, sliding.

"Yes, he's fine. Watch yourself. Don't come too fast."

I met the troopers partway down. "Where did you find him?"

"You won't believe it. We found him sitting in a pile of leaves, half covered with them, not more than five feet from the trail, just beyond the brook. We'd been by the spot a half a dozen times before; he must have heard us calling but just didn't answer. It was almost as though he didn't want us to find him. Anyway, when we went back to the brook again we flashed the light around and the beam hit his face, white as a ghost in the night, and his blond hair and we knew we had him."

Ah, Matthew, I think—and there is something in me that sorrows, as if at the capture of a deer or fox or some other wild thing—I wish that there were some way that I could set you free. You must have gotten cold. I could see it so clearly: Matt covering his bare legs with the leaves, sitting silently, silently, as the troopers tramped back and forth.

"Was he all right? What did he do?"

"He's fine. The other teacher, the big fellow, has him in the car. They're waiting for you. We came back to tell you we'd found him. Only thing we couldn't find was his shoe. He lost one of his shoes; must be in the leaves. But he wasn't hurt. Matter of fact, didn't even seem scared. He was laughing when we found him. Just sitting there laughing."

They walk with me to the parking lot, outlining the trail with their flashlights, and then when the bus comes in view they leave and I walk the rest of the way across the lot by moonlight. They are sitting there, Dan and Matt, in the front seat, and Dan leans across Matt and opens the door for me.

"You okay, Junior?" Dan's face looks very tired in the thin light.

I get in and the three of us sit looking at each other wordlessly.

Finally, Matt leans his head tentatively against my shoulder and I put my arm around him, and we drive like that, the three of us in the front seat, Dan and me, Matthew between us.

We didn't talk. All the things we had to say were too big for words.

Chapter *TWELVE*

"I don't know anything at all about team teaching," I say to Dan.

"You're an expert."

"How's that? How did I get to be an expert?"

"Because it's just what we've been doing the last couple of months, combining our classes, except that next year we'll be in the same classroom all the time. One big room for eight kids instead of two small ones. See, the thing is this. Doris wants to bring in six more kids—two more for you plus one more teacher and four kids. And if you and I combine in the big room, that will free one of the rooms for the new class."

"And our room? What will that be like?" I ask, trying to get a picture.

"It'll be good. Open. The kids can work in small groups; we'll have two aides each morning, so that will be four of us. We can get a science project going—art, reading, math—and the kids can move back and forth between the groups. Freedom in a structured setting."

"Where's the structure?"

"Us. We're structured. We believe in the same things, the same kind of discipline, responsibility. We let the kids grow at their own pace, provide the materials and help if they need it; let them test themselves with us . . . For God's sake, I can't put it in words . . . you know what I mean."

I did. I knew.

"What does Doris think?" I asked.

"She's all for it. She wants more kids, hopes eventually to have room for forty in the new building. Besides—more kids, more money."

"Dan. That's not fair." This was one of the few things we disagreed about: the Director. Dan was antagonistic toward her, whereas I felt an increasing respect for this woman who had managed to found the school and keep it operating for thirteen years. And her dream was coming closer. There was an architect's rendering now of the new building. Formal fund-raising was starting. Dan found her stubborn, unwilling to change; he disliked the way she said one thing one day, another the next, agreeing with the psychologist during staff meetings, disagreeing with him after he left.

To me—she survived. And kept us all surviving with her. There was tremendous strength inside her slender body and she used every ounce of it, playing the odds, swaying back and forth, it's true, like a tree in a storm, this way toward the board of trustees, back to the teachers, leaning toward the professionals, bending to the parents; but this was her secret of survival. The pressures upon her were incredible. She could not remain rigid or she would be felled. She was strange about money, fishing old broken crayons out of the wastebasket, cutting up partly used paper for scraps. But she used the scraps. She sacrificed for her dream—the new school.

Dan was not concerned with some future dream: he was young, he was interested in now. He wanted good conditions, good supplies of materials for his kids right now. Why should they, his boys, suffer for some old woman's distant dream?

Dan's other complaint was that Doris did not visit the classrooms enough, was not in close enough touch with the children, the teachers. She was not, he said, aware of what we were doing and trying to do. Consequently, Dan, like a child himself, felt that if she didn't care enough to find out, he had no obligation to inform her.

But again the fact remained: we did survive, and more than that, we grew. Through all our crises, big and small—in spite of ourselves. Matthew on the mountain, for instance, could have been a tragedy, but wasn't. Now in some strange way our classes were closer than ever. We had known fear and not been torn apart by it; we had made mistakes and not turned on each other. Matthew was no longer so wild; when we crossed even the small street to the graveyard he came and put his hand into mine, never looking at me—but our hands clasped as we crossed the street.

In any event, for once Dan and Doris both wanted the same thing, though for different reasons. Doris wanted more children; Dan wanted to try the concept of team teaching. Whatever my reservations were, they seemed small in the face of their united decision.

"All right," I said, "let's try it."

The last days of school were hot. We worked hard, conscious of trying to prepare the children for summer, give them as many skills, as much self-reliance, as we could, then staying late in the afternoon, planning for the next year. It was hard to say good-bye. Tired as we all were, we had grown used to each other and were conscious of how much we would miss one another.

We had a final party in place of the usual staff meeting. We held it in Jerry Cramer's backyard, out on the flagstone terrace, overlooking a long meadow filled with apple trees and bordered by low stone walls. The terrace faced west and the late afternoon sun hung over the low range of mountains that rose at the end of the meadow.

Jerry was our psychiatric social worker; he was also a psychologist. He spent more time at the school than the other professionals, often without pay. He had a long, soft, gray mustache, steel-rimmed glasses, and a gentle manner. Though he had his human failings (always trying to stop smoking, which never lasted more than a day), he loved the children and they knew it. They would often go of their own volition to stand beside him or sit near him at Circle.

Dr. Marino, our psychiatrist, was there too. Reserved, always at a slight distance from all of us, but able, informed; I wished there was some way that he could spend more time at the school.

There was no shop talk that day, only gentle jokes and reminiscences. Zoe drank martinis and sat on the the flagstone terrace like a small guru. Only our speech pathologist was absent.

I knew I must go—Rick's high-school graduation was that night—but the tenderness I had felt all year had risen to the surface, floating on Jerry's bourbon, and it was difficult for me to leave these people. I kissed Zoe and hugged Doris, surprised at myself; I was not usually a woman hugger.

Then Dan walked me to my car parked in front of the house, opened the door for me and waited while I found the key and put it in the ignition.

"How about working with me this summer, Mair? I've already got eight kids signed up for the summer program and there are a lot more prospects. I'll need help. How about it?"

I wanted to. Rick was driving cross-country with friends before college; Elizabeth had been asked back to camp as a junior counselor. I wanted the work, the children, the closeness—but I had problems to resolve in my marriage; I could not retreat from them into the joy of teaching.

I turn on the ignition, and regret makes my voice formal. "Thank you, Dan, but I can't. I've made other commitments." And the word stands formal and strange between us.

Dan leans his arms on the edge of the car window and bends his big frame until his eyes are only an inch from mine, and I turn my head away before I say, "Good-bye, Dan. Good luck. I'll see you in the fall."

He leans there looking at me, not moving, holding the car door, and then finally he straightens, "Take care, Junior. Take care of yourself this summer."

I left then and drove down the highway in the heat of the late afternoon, but before I have gone a mile I pull to the side of the road and put up the top of my convertible. Even with the heat I put the top up, and put my own polished shell back on as well.

Chapter THIRTEEN

I went to the marriage counselor alone. I tried to persuade Larry to come with me, but he said it was ridiculous because there was nothing wrong. I thought perhaps it was true—it might be ridiculous, but for the opposite reason: everything was so wrong it could not be put right.

I sat opposite the tall, distinguished psychiatrist—shy, not knowing what to say, intimidated by the black leather couch on the outer rim of my vision. Will he ask me to lie down?

"Yes . . . ?" he says.

I try to tell him about all the good things and the bad. My voice seems far away. I can hear it while I am talking, and it is almost as though I am speaking about another person. I talk about our children—and Larry's and my good physical relationship, and the lovely house and tennis—but when I try to tell him about the bad parts, I find I cannot talk about them very well; all the reserve I was taught as a child, the New England sense of privacy, wells up and sorrow fills my throat.

"Humph. Now. So. Do you think you are beautiful?"

Surprise makes me raise my head and look at him. "No," I say. "No."

All angular and lean is Dr. McPhearson, but now he smiles at me, a slow, kind smile and I like him suddenly.

"Ahhrph." This man has his noises, too, not so different from the children. "So. Well, do you feel you are intelligent?"

"A little. Some. I can think better than I can talk."

It is easier to talk now, and I tell him more. How it will not be as difficult to live with Larry with the children gone next year, Rick to college, Elizabeth to Kent. How we never fight, Larry and myself—how if I could just be content with the things I have, it would probably be all right; but there seems to be so much emptiness. And then, there is all this love, and I don't know what to do with it. Larry doesn't really want it. I don't blame him—it's too much. It gets too much for me too. I get all filled up with it and I have to let it out. Do you think maybe it's like too much fat—that it could be slimmed down?

"The school," he suggests.

"Yes. I am good at that," I say. "I love teaching there, but, I don't know—it's hard to say it—but you see, anyone could do that. I mean either a man or a woman could do that kind of loving and it's—the school is—good for that part; but there's this other part of me that loves only like a woman. This part is for a man. I love being a woman . . ."

He takes off his glasses and smiles again, a small, tired smile.

"Yes," he says. "Can your husband come with you next time?"

Larry almost came, but then he was detained at his bank in the city and so I go alone again. This time we talk about the laser: Light Amplification by Stimulated Emission of Radiation. Delicate, intricate, powerful. Energy harnessed from a larger source. Is it possible that love could be like this?

On the fifth visit he says unexpectedly, "What will you do if you leave your husband?"

"I'll teach."

"And how will you live? Who will take care of you? Have you ever lived alone?"

It seems amazing to me. I realize I never have. I have never spent a night alone. First my parents—overnights with friends—college, roommates—Larry—my parents when he was in the army—the children.

"No," I say. "Not really. But I am sure that I can learn."

Dr. McPhearson called Larry and arranged an appointment, and Larry went first alone and then with me. He explained carefully to Dr. McPhearson how there was nothing wrong, that I tended to be too sensitive, imagine things.

I sat silently, listening, shrinking, getting smaller again.

"Hrrmph. Ah. Mmph." Dr. McPhearson clears his throat, and the familiar noises cheer me. "Well, Mary. What do you say?"

"I am going"—sounding stubborn, I knew, unreasoning—but it would take so little. It would be so easy to stay.

Dr. McPhearson recommends that I take a trip. Living alone is different from thinking about it, he says. Larry is enthusiastic. Just what she needs, he says—a trip, to get away from it all. He likes the doctor, and I am glad. He will need someone to talk to.

I go for one more visit.

"Ahhh," he says, even before we begin. "I am sorry. Perhaps if you had come ten years ago . . ."

I shake his hand before I go. Is that how you say good-bye to a psychiatrist?

"Thank you," I say, "for all your time."

"Yahrmph." A combination of yes and throat-clearing. "Is there anything more? Anything I can do? Where will you be?"

"California, I think. I've never been there."

He stands silently.

"There is one other thing," I say. "The guilt. I feel a big ball of guilt . . . Here." I touch my stomach. "Is there anything I can do about that?"

"Guilt. Why is that? What do you mean, guilt?"

It is so difficult to tell him and I think again how hard it is to communicate through words, and I marvel to myself that we all do as well as we do. We are all interpreters by necessity, even though we are not trained or suited for the profession. Simultaneous interpreters, hearing one language and then speaking another, our own. Ahh, we need more tolerance, more admiration for one another.

"I feel guilty about leaving him alone. Who will make the coffee in the morning or put flowers in the silver bowl? And the animals, will they be all right? How will Larry know how to order the meat or which slipcovers to send to the cleaner's? He doesn't know how to work the dryer or where I packed his winter things . . ." I stop in confusion.

"You are not his mother, Mary."

And I want to say, I know, I know, and yet, part of me is. Just as I can see separate parts of me, parts that are satisfied working with the children and other parts that are man-oriented, so I also see blended centers of me. Where does the mother end and the lover begin? Which is student, which teacher? Is being a wife supposed to be a separate, isolate thing? I do not think it can be.

But before I can speak again Dr. McPhearson interrupts my thoughts. "It will be all right," he says. "It is like grief—the guilt—you must just work it through."

Chapter FOURTEEN

Coming in from the hot June air, I notice that the halls of the school are cool and dark, strangely quiet and empty without the children. The Director is there, though, talking on the phone, and she waves as I walk through her office on the way to my classroom.

There are books and papers I want to take with me to California, and I had thought merely to drop by the school and pick them up. I had not realized how strange the school would seem without the children, and now as I kneel in front of the small white bookcase thumbing the speech manual, images of Brian and Matthew superimpose themselves upon the pages and I cannot concentrate.

The Director's voice floats down the hall, echoing in the silent spaces: "I think it's going to come out all right, Arthur. I've just gone over the books again and I've made a list of the most urgent bills. Yes. I know. There are quite a few, but a lot of them we can stall until fall. We'll be all right then; the school boards will be sending in half of the tuition."

Arthur must be Arthur Siegal, the school's accountant, Doris's cohort in fighting the never-ending battle against the drain of money.

"Yes, all right. I can give you the list of the ones I've marked most urgent now, but I'd like to get together with you soon, get these things paid before I leave. You didn't? Oh . . . Guatemala. No, no, just for the summer, teaching in one of the colleges. I'll be back in the fall."

Doris reads off a list of names and amounts, including bills from the phone and electric companies. "No. Skip that. Leave it until fall."

Irritation now in her voice, no cheeriness, just irritation and weariness.

"Arthur. Look. I told you—I don't need it. I know I didn't get last month's salary either; I can read the books as well as you. But I don't need it. I've got my ticket in my pocketbook, groceries till the end of the week, and I'll get an advance when I get there.

"The Board meeting is Thursday night, you know that, and I want to be in the black. I mean I want the school to be in the black. When you read the figures to the Board, I want them to look good, positive. The Board's enthusiastic now; the fund-raising for the new school is moving right along. If they think we've gone in the hole they'll let down, get discouraged.

"Mmmm. Right. Well, that's your job, Arthur. You print up the sheets so they don't notice my salary's not there.

"All right. Good. Thanks a million. See you tomorrow then."

Chris and Brad and Tom and Billy, Ivan and Jeffy, and more, more. All the children of the school join the images of Brian and Matt; all the children Doris has made room for, all the problems she faces without complaint.

Unexpectedly, she appears in the doorway of my small classroom. "Mary, how are you? Can I help you with anything?"

"No," I say. "I'm just picking up some books to go over during the summer. Did I hear that you're going to Guatemala?"

She sits down quickly on one of the tables; her

bright brown eyes move over my face as if to read me, to see how much else I have heard.

"Yes; I've been there before. I've found it's good to get away, get a change of scene during the summer."

We sit quietly, Doris and I, in the dim classroom until she says, "Fourteen years now since I opened the school. We started with just four children—half a day."

"How did you know about them? How did you think to open a school for emotionally disturbed children?"

"Well, you know, when you look back, it's strange how it happened. The parents really began the school. They got the idea, four of them, and then came to me and asked if I'd be in charge.

"I'd done all kinds of things when I was younger. Then I began teaching and it turned out that I had a knack with the 'problems,' as the other teachers called them, and one thing led to another, and the next thing I knew, there we were starting the school.

"Harry ... well, I wish you could have known him. He supported me all the way, baby-sat at night with Mike while I got my master's, built furniture for the school, painted walls. I didn't marry until late, but he was worth waiting for. I could never have started the school or kept it going without him.

"I remember right in the beginning, fifteen years ago, saying to him, 'Harry, I don't know anything about emotionally disturbed children,' and him saying, 'Well, Doris, it doesn't sound to me like anybody else knows either, and at least you admit it.' "

I smile at Doris; she makes it seem so real. I can almost picture Harry.

"We built our own house, you know, little by little. Bought the property, then put it up a room at a time, and while we were measuring or painting or laying the bricks I'd tell him about the children. He knew each one as well as I did, and he helped me a lot more than anybody else. Had a listening heart, Harry did."

Doris is quiet for a while; I can almost hear her listening to me, though neither of us is speaking. If Helga and I have a body language, Doris has an inner ear and she somehow knows things long before they are put into words.

Now she says, "I was a funny kid. Always bringing home sick cats or birds with broken wings; had a regular clinic in the backyard of our house when I was young. I must have nearly driven my mother crazy, but she never said a word until the summer I brought home Leland Hagstrom. He was handsome as anything, but weak—drank like a fish, couldn't seem to leave the bottle alone. After supper one night that summer my mother took me out on the back porch and asked me how serious I was about Leland. I was pretty serious; he needed me, or said he did—and I liked that.

"I'd never lied to her and it didn't occur to me to do it then, so I told her the truth, that we were thinking of getting married. You know what she said? 'You're a fool if you do, Doris. I'm not one to interfere, but remember'—and I've never forgotten this—'remember,' she said, 'never do your social work at home.' "

Doris sighs and gets off the table. "Well, I didn't marry Leland. I waited, and after a while I met Harry and we had a love affair that lasted thirty years . . . I don't know what made me think of it now; I must be getting old, rambling on like this. Well now, you get to work, don't let me keep you. Where are you off to for vacation?"

"Oh," I say, "California, I think."

"It's a beautiful state; you'll like it. Have a good

summer now; I probably won't see you until fall."
Another cheery wave and Doris disappeared out the
door.

I finished gathering my books and papers, thinking all the while about Doris. Had she just been
rambling on or in her own way had she been giving
me advice? In any event, before I went home I drove
five miles beyond the school and put a deposit on
one of the new apartments that would be completed
in the fall.

Chapter *FIFTEEN*

I am back from California and settled in my new apartment a week before school opens. The apartment is small and there is not much furniture, but it is carpeted in gold and open on both sides so that the morning sun pours through the bedroom and living room and the afternoon light fills the small kitchen and dining room.

Larry's and my separation is complete, the final papers signed; only the formality of the divorce remains, and this has been postponed until January for tax purposes.

Elizabeth and Rick are back in school, tanned and healthy from the summer, and my own impatience to begin work, to see the children, wells inside me.

Bedlam. The first day in our new room is bedlam and Dan and I barely have a chance to speak to each other. Eight children in the room. Supposedly four are mine and four Dan's, but we can never remember exactly who is whose.

Brian is back, taller, still flapping.

"Hey, Bri, did you have a good summer?"

"Mary. Mary. Is your father dead?"

What is this now? "No. My father isn't dead. Why?"

"Where does he live?"

"In Guilford, Connecticut."

"Yule O'Toole lives in Guilford."

132

"Who is Yule O'Toole?"

"Yule O'Toole is dead. I thought maybe you were dead, too—the summer was so long."

"Not me, Bri. I'm going to be around for a long time. I've got a lot to catch up on." Later I found out that Brian's grandfather had died during the summer.

Stuart comes sliding in the door.

"You look perfectly darling this fall, Mary."

"Thank you, Stuart. I'm glad to see you."

"Shit," he says and kisses my hand, licking it with his tongue. Jeffy Olivero and his widowed mother have disappeared without a trace over the summer, and I wonder if he still sleeps beside her, pressing her earlobe between his thumb and forefinger, wherever they may be.

Tom and Ivan, Dan's boys from the year before, are back; the new room is strange to them and Ivan whirls and jumps in one corner, his beautiful face a silent mask, while Tom pulls up his turtleneck and paces back and forth along the wall.

"Good morning, Tom," I say.

"Good morning, Tom. Goddamn fucking son of a bitch. Lost on the mountain. Call the one o'clock call."

And I know that he remembers me, although I am not so sure that he is glad to see me in this new room. Changes are difficult for all children; for ours, they are doubly so. Their own self-image is so fragile that any alteration in the immediate external environment is a major threat.

If it is hard for the returning children, it is even harder for the four new ones, two boys and two girls.

Tony, seven years old, black eyes bright, perches on a table beside me. "Kee-rist. What a bunch of weirdoes." Tony's mother ran away when she discovered she was pregnant again, and he lives now in a single motel room with his father and his father's mistress. Before the morning is out I am extracting a five-dollar bill that he is transferring from my purse to the inside of his shoe. When I take it back, Tony yells in rage. "See. I knew it. I knew it. You goddamn whore. No matter what you look like, you're mean. Mean. Like all the rest of them."

Alice is the first girl for either of us. She is twelve, with tight blond braids and angry, slanted eyes. She spends the first hour drawing at the blackboard as the others arrive, drawing huge ice cream cones, labeling in careful letters each mound of ice cream . . . vanilla breast . . . chocolate breast . . . butter pecan breast. Twenty-seven flavors?

Dan asks her what she's doing and she says, "Shut up. I want my own way in the world. Why can't I have my own way in the world?"

"You better take her," says Dan. "She seems to need a maternal influence."

"Thanks a lot," I say.

Jenny Woodriff is our second and only other girl. She isn't new; she had been in Renée's class, but neither Dan nor I had known her well. She is eight but seems much smaller because she walks doubled over, hands almost touching the ground. Her auburn curly hair is pulled down over her eyes, hiding most of her face. She doesn't speak; she only barks. Jenny thinks she is a dog.

"She's for me," says Dan.

"Aw, come on. You're making all the decisions."

"Okay, okay. You get to pick the next one."

Rufus stands in the doorway dressed like a middle-aged businessman, blue suit, necktie, glasses, large briefcase held in front of his fat stomach.

"I am Rufus Jay Greenberg," he announces. "I live at Six-eight-nine Harrison Avenue. You may call me Rufus, or Rufus Jay—or if you are very angry, Rufus Jay Greenberg."

"Come on in, Rufus," I say.

Rufus extends his hand, warm, moist, pudgy, and says, "Is that what you are going to call me?"

"I guess so. Would that be okay? What do your friends call you?"

For the first time he looks up and I can see the nystagmus that moves his eyes rapidly back and forth, back and forth, like the carriage on a typewriter.

"I don't have any friends," he says.

He spreads his arms wide, the briefcase still dangling from his right hand, and sails to the farthest corner of the room. He pulls a wooden toy chest away from the wall and squats behind it, arms wrapped around his briefcase.

Rufus is eight. His family moved to the area so that Rufus could attend our school. Both his mother and father had given up good jobs to make the move, she as a teacher, he as a chemist in a large pharmaceutical firm. Rufus had been in a "special school" in Pennsylvania and, because of the family's educational and chemical-medical background, had been tested and retested. Rufus' file is thicker than the rest of my children's put together. He has been given tests by psychologists, psychiatrists, neurologists, in major cities all over the East. Each report differs from the next:—"normal intelligence with emotional disturbance"—"retarded"—"brain-injured" —"normal to bright normal with schizophrenic tendencies."

How could there be so many different opinions? No wonder the parents were discouraged and Rufus himself had an absentee record that was higher than the days he had attended school.

"I want him," I say to Dan.

Brian's bright, pointed little face contorts with un-happiness. He copes with jealousy by accelerating his flapping and uttering the old-time squawk. "Awk, awk. Gonna go to the doctor's."

Finally we are all there, the six boys—Dan's Tom and Ivan from last year, my own Brian (Matthew is in a neurologically impaired class in a public school) and Stuart, and now the two new boys, Rufus and Tony, and the two girls, Alice and Jenny.

We had our own circle now, the eight children— Tom, Ivan, Tony, Jenny Woodriff, Brian, Stuart, Alice, Rufus—and of course Dan and me. Dan ran our circle but it was not called "Circle" anymore. Dan referred to it as "opening exercises." "Circle is a baby name," he said. "You can't treat these kids like babies and then expect them to act like eight- or ten- or twelve-year-old kids."

We saluted the flag and sang "America the Beautiful." Of course, only Dan and I sang, and I have a very small, off-key voice so it was really only Dan, but he sang with gusto. And when we had finished singing about America he got out his guitar and sang "A Frog He Did A-courtin' Go" and "He's Got the Whole World in His Hands."

By the end of the second week Stuart began to sing with us in a high, clear tenor. Neither of us had ever heard him sing before, but now he was totally absorbed. Feet off the ground, legs stretched straight out in front of him, eyes fixed on a distant point, hands moving in some ritual before his face, Stuart sang. He knew the words, he knew the tune. Across his head, Dan and I exchanged looks of satisfaction.

It was not so easy with some of the others. Ivan never uttered a word and Dan saluted the flag with one arm around him to stop his constant whirling. The flag excited Ivan, and it was not until we appointed him flag-bearer that he stood still and stared in fascination at the flag he held. Jenny Woodriff didn't sing, of course. At first she refused to sit, pushing the chair away and squatting on the floor, her hands curled in front of her chest like a small dog begging. Dan would not let her stay there: he lifted her up and put her in the chair—"Hey, bear, keep your bottom on the chair"—and held her there while she yelped in fury. Gradually she relaxed and one day she sat, leaning her small body against Dan as he strummed his guitar. When he sang directly to her, " 'Miss Mousie, will you marry me? Mm-hmm, Mm-hmm,' " I was certain that a smile was not very far away.

Beside me that first day of school, Alice clutched the seat of her chair with both hands and pounded it against the floor, filled with rage at having to leave her ice cream breasts. Between clenched teeth she muttered, "I want my own way," and suddenly she stood up and flung the chair across the room, barely missing Rufus. Dan sat quietly, looking not at Alice but at me, and I knew this was mine to handle. I knew that Dan was thinking that I must set the limits now, establish my own relationship with this strange, tormented girl. He would help me if I needed it, but he would not do it for me.

I stand, too, and look at Alice. "What's wrong? Tell me. Can you tell me?" Alice snarls some curse and then spits directly in my face.

"Chairs are for sitting," I say. "Get it, please, and bring it back," and I let the spittle remain upon my cheek. Tears suddenly burst out of Alice, and she goes and leans against the wall and puts her head against her arm. I follow and turn her from the wall and put my arms around her, and Dan keeps singing, ". . . little bitty baby in His arms, He's got the whole world in His arms."

"Come on now," I say finally. "Let's get the chair and go back," and Alice goes and brings it back and we both sit down again.

Within a month, however, our opening exercises have gained form and structure, incidents of this kind are rare, and everyone is singing except Ivan and Jenny Woodriff.

Directly after these opening exercises we have our academics. In those first few days of the new term I think often of Matthew and wonder how he is doing in the new neurologically impaired class that has been established in his home town. I miss his blond head, but I am glad he qualified for the class. His speech had been coming faster and faster in those last days and I feel sure that he will get the help he needs.

I am going to school three nights a week now, driving down to the State Teachers College, taking courses called Introduction to the Handicapped, a prerequisite for all other courses; Teaching the Socially Maladjusted and the Emotionally Disturbed; and Art in Special Education. I attended faithfully and finally earned three As, but my disappointment in the courses became disillusionment when they asked me to give three lectures on the emotionally disturbed. Ah, Helga, how much more I learned from you.

Helga taught me first to begin where the child is. Never assume—always find out. In more academic language this means diagnose, teach, diagnose, teach. Never go blindly on from lesson plan to lesson plan, as they seemed to suggest at college, with so much talk of lesson plans, unit teaching, curriculum planning. Which of those professors had been in a class like ours, I wondered?

My job, as I saw it, was to teach the children how to live within homes and communities. If what I taught contributed to that, good; if not, it was a waste. The children obviously had to learn self-help and certain social skills. They had to learn how to adapt their behavior so that it would be acceptable to the society in which they lived. They could not, for instance, continue to spit or masturbate in public; these actions would earn them ridicule or isolation, and they must be taught to control them or substitute other, more acceptable behavior.

This aspect of teaching is first and foremost. We must first reach the children, reach through the rage and fear and hate, before we can teach. This is why we are called therapeutic teachers.

However, I did not believe in basket-weaving.

Unless, of course, you happened to love basket-weaving above all else. For me, it was communication: the give-and-take between people—spoken, written, however it came—and I wanted to give my children the chance to learn these things. I had read their records, their testing; all of it was sketchy, but every indication was that they were of normal intellectual ability, or above. They deserved to be allowed to learn the techniques of communication.

The other teachers thought I was somewhat ambitious. They were kind and encouraging, but it did not have the same importance for them as it did for me. And yet, and yet, if what I loved and wished to teach was reading, I had as much right to teach that as potato-printing. In the children's world of violent emotion, where everything continually changes, I thought it would be satisfying for them to know that some things remain constant. A C is a C both today and tomorrow—and C-A-T remains "cat" through tears and violence.

I began with the alphabet, in spite of the fact that Brian and Alice could already read. It wouldn't do them any harm, and it was necessary to teach below their level so that we could function as a group. I taught them each the twenty-six symbols of our language. First to recognize them, then gradually to make them and know their sounds.

I would line the chalk tray with letters printed on cards and ask the children to bring me a D, a B or an F. As soon as they learned these, I asked them to make the letter on the board. Within the month Alice and Brian were making up their own words, Stuart could write most of the alphabet. Rufus was just beginning.

"Can you find the D, Rufus?"

Down goes his head onto one of the tables we use as desks.

"Here now, let's see. I will make a D on the board. A big one, see? The straight line—then the fat stomach. Okay, now. D. Can you see a letter like this?"

I nudge the D card more prominently into view—and slowly, slowly, Rufus gets up from behind his desk and comes forward to where I stand. I take his finger and trace it over the D on the board, saying, "Here's that D, Ruf. Like in 'Dog.' Feel here, see how it's made." I am trying to imprint the letter in his mind. But his body is tight with fear and when he goes to the chalk tray of cards to pick out the D, he just stands looking at them blankly. And I know that the major problem here is that Rufus is too frightened to commit himself to a choice, terrified that he may pick the wrong letter.

Finally a way out of the situation occurs to him, and he walks across the front of the room trailing his finger against the ledge of the chalk tray where the alphabet cards rest, his eyes fastened on me rather than the cards.

What is this now? Suddenly I understand. In his own way he is asking for help, and when he goes back and does it again, his eyes still on me rather than the cards, I wait. I wait until his finger touches the card marked D and then I say, "Yes, Good! That's it. Good, Rufus." And he looks down and picks up the card and brings it to me.

He looks at it carefully as he hands it to me.

"Is that right, Mary? Did I get it right?"

"Exactly right, Rufus. Good. That's a D."

His eyes focus on the letter, and the blank, scared look is gone. For an instant, at least, fear is forgotten and learning can take place.

Two weeks later when I ask for a Q and start to draw one on the board for him to trace, he walks straight to the Q and hands it to me, saying, "Who needs that baby stuff on the board?"

"Okay, fine, Rufus," is all I say. But inside I feel that fine surge of excitement that says, "He's going now. He's off the ground. We're moving."

One thing I was certain of concerning Rufus. He was half paralyzed with fear. The ambiguity of the testing seemed somewhat more understandable to me after the first few days. Certainly not knowing the alphabet at eight years of age was below normal achievement. But what was the cause? Was it lack of capacity? Or was there something blocking the potential?

Inside myself I bet on a good average intelligence for Rufus. The phrasing of his sentences, his mannerisms, all belied retardation; it seemed more likely to me that there was some neurological impairment, some tiny section of the pathways of input and output that didn't function properly, and that this imperfection had caused poor performance and, on occasion, failure. When you have failed often and painfully enough you will do almost anything to avoid having to try again. But I was sure—I knew—that he could learn to compensate if I could reach him. What I was trying to do was to remove his blockades of fear so that I could get through. I knew my best chance was through success. As a construction crew bulldozes through a jungle, so I tried to bulldoze my way through Rufus' fears. Calculate how far he'd come, open up the situation to the degree where success was ensured—then get him to try.

The main difficulty was trying to teach on widely spread levels and keep everyone interested and learning.

As Rufus hands me an M, I say to Brian, "Give me a word that begins with M, Brian."

"Mother," he says.

"Good. Spell it, Alice."

"M-o-t-h-e-r."

"Okay, fine. Use it in a sentence, Stu."

"My mother won't let me play with light bulbs," says Stuart.

"Why?" asks Alice, interested. And we talk about this. Alice is fascinated that there is someone else who cannot have his own way in the world.

"What do you mean, why? I don't know why. She just says I can't play with them."

"But why not? I mean, what's the matter with light bulbs?" Alice's voice is gentler than I've ever heard it. She's honestly interested in another person.

Stuart is impatient, though. His eyebrows raise like owl eyes behind his steel-rimmed glasses.

"Jesus. Stupid," he says. "How many kids do you see building houses out of light bulbs in their boxes?"

But Alice only sighs. "They're nice and round," she says. And I can almost see her matching ice cream breast for light bulb in her head.

There are no easy answers here; at least not for me. I have no way of knowing what ice cream breasts and light bulbs mean to Alice and Stuart. All I know is that these things are part of them, as much a part of them as the way they stand or speak. And that the most important thing that I can do right now is accept them. Accept each child as an individual, the way he is—ice cream breasts, light bulbs, and all. And maybe in this atmosphere of accepting and trusting each other we can grow a little more.

Finally, I decided we were ready for a series of books. I inspected all the different series, finally deciding on "Science Research Associates," liking the physical production, the linguistic approach in the basic series, the wide range of speed and comprehension in the laboratory level. It would be good for all the children, and the workbooks were sufficiently self-explanatory that the children could work on them independently while I worked with each of them individually for a short period of time. And the teachers' manual was clear enough so that the aides could follow it.

I told Dan of my decision.

"You'll have a devil of a time getting her to spend the money," he said.

"I'm going to bring it up at staff meeting; I don't see how she can refuse."

"Good luck," Dan said.

I take the catalog with pictures and description to staff meeting and pass it around.

"I am sure the children can learn to read," I say. "But they need a programmed series so that they can progress from level to level, building their skills."

Doris says, "In my experience, teacher-made material is much more effective."

"I agree," I answer. "And I would supplement the series with other material that I supply. But I cannot write a whole series of textbooks for kindergarten through sixth grade in the next week, and they're ready to learn now."

"Perhaps you should have thought of that this summer." Doris smiles at me. "Meanwhile, the Ladies' Association of the church did donate a whole carton of books to us, and I noticed just the other day that there were two *Cowboy Sams* among them. They're excellent, you know. Excellent."

I look down in frustration and notice that Dan is scribbling on a piece of paper beside me.

"The way I figure it," he says, "is that we've got eight kids in our room and the last I heard, tuition here was three thousand dollars a year—that's twenty-four thousand dollars just in our room. Of course, you've got the heat and light bills. I know the church only donates the building—then, too, there are our salaries . . ."

Quickly the Director interrupts. Dan said later she was ashamed to have my small salary of four thousand disclosed.

"What did you say the series would cost, Mary?"

"One hundred and eighty-six dollars for one of each, plus mailing," and I wonder as I say it if she knows I probably love and respect her more than anyone else in the room. And yet I must fight her for what I believe right . . .

"The expenditure seems reasonable enough," says Dr. Marino, our psychiatrist.

"It isn't the money," says Doris. "It's simply that it is foolish to buy too much material while we are here. It will be such a job to transport it all to the new building, the new school. But, I suppose . . . if you're sure it will be thoroughly used . . ."

"I'll be glad to carry the box to the new building," says Dan.

I kick him under the table.

"Thank you," I say to the Director. "It will be used, I promise."

Later in the parking lot I say to Dan, "You're the

one I really thank. You got me the books. Of course, you almost ruined it too . . . 'I'll be glad to carry the box,' " I mimic.

"She makes me so goddamn mad. That school isn't going to be finished for at least two years, if ever, and already she's using it as an excuse."

"Anyway," I say, "thank you. I really appreciate it."

Chapter SIXTEEN

We are being observed all the time now. At first we—the children and myself—were self-conscious when three, four, sometimes five, visitors stood in the back of the classroom watching. But now we are so totally absorbed in each other and what we're doing that we barely notice them. The door opens and they file to the back of the classroom and the Director waves from the door.

Dan is annoyed when Zoe reports that Doris includes a talk about "our marvelous experiment in team teaching ... the phenomenal success we've had," in her public relations sessions.

"We?" he shouts. "What does she mean, 'we'? She never even puts her ass in the door. Just waves everybody else in and then stands there and wiggles her fingers. She doesn't have any idea what we're doing."

It was true that word had spread about the school, the team teaching, and the reading, and the visitors were increasing in all the classes. Each day of the week there would be some group—other teachers, doctors, students, Junior Leaguers, psychiatric nurses, occasionally nuns from the St. Francis Guild.

I loved the nuns with their black robes and gentle hands and faces. I had worked in a Catholic hospital during two summers of my adolescence, and their quiet ways had made a lasting impression on me.

There were four nuns there the day that Tony

shocked them. Tony, small and sturdy, with his rough thatch of black hair and broad, short, little body, was doing well in Dan's group, although both Dan and I felt he was incorrectly placed in our school. He was nowhere near sick enough. There was none of the weird behavior, either aggressive or withdrawn, that characterized the other children. He stole; he lied; he cheated—but he was not out of touch with reality. However, his own school district had refused to accept him in their public school system, saying he was seriously emotionally disturbed, and somehow our staff had accepted him.

Tony seemed to us more lonely than disturbed. Because he had not been allowed in school, he had spent his days wandering the streets or sitting alone in the cheap motel room while his father and girl friend worked and the school board sought "suitable placement" for him. Consequently, he loved being in our school—the singing, the trips, the activities—although he stared with wide eyes at the bizarre behavior of the other children. And now he was beginning to learn to read, and he loved that even more. Although he was technically one of Dan's children, he joined my group for academics and was both a pleasure and a chore: he cheated whenever possible, stole whatever he could get away with, and conned the other innocents.

"Mary, Mary. Look at Tony. He's got Brian's car." And Brian would be flapping. "Tony. Tony. Give it back. Dead. Dead. Mary, is the car dead?"

Finally Tony would stop running in circles and take the car out of his pocket and toss it on the desk and say, "Here, baby. Who wants a stupid car anyway?"

Tony was tough; he was also scared. He sat next to me at lunch and in the car when he could, and walked closely by my side through the park. He never mentioned his mother, who had left suddenly—only a note one morning that she was pregnant again—and had gone South to her family. That was over a year ago and there had been no further word. Tony's father had moved out of the project where they had lived and taken his girl friend and Tony to the motel room—one room for three.

The day the nuns were there, Tony had read his first full sentence out loud and was bursting with excitement.

"Ya gonna tell my father? Hey, Mair, are ya? You gonna tell him how good I can read?"

"You bet I am. I'm not only going to tell him; I'm going to show him. Right here in the book."

Tony comes close to me then. We are putting on our jackets to go outside for a minute before lunch, and the nuns move forward to thank us, to ask a question.

Suddenly Tony's arms go around my waist and his small face looks up at me intently. "Hey, Mary? Can I screw you?" he says loudly, clearly.

I knew what he meant. He meant, "I love you." He meant, "I love being able to read, and love you because you helped." I knew that probably the only affection or expression of love that he witnessed in the motel room was couched in such phrases; he was only using the words that he had heard.

I heard one nun gasp; another covered her mouth.

And I smiled at them over Tony's head as I hugged him back and said, "You gotta wait a few years, Tony. I'm a little old for you." I was sorry to shock the gentle nuns, but I had to do what I would have done had they not been there.

Outside, Tony ran ahead toward our baseball field in the graveyard, carrying the bat, and Dan said, "Goddamn it, that was great. You kept your cool, Junior. You could have tried to look good in front of the nuns, but instead you heard him, you really heard him."

I am pleased to be praised for something so easy. But Dan will not let me bask comfortably in his praise. He tosses our baseball in the air and catches it under his knee, grins at me, and says, "How about me? Can I . . . ?"

It was working. The idea of team teaching for seriously disturbed kids was proving itself. The therapeutic milieu that psychiatrists speak of was in our classroom. It was a place where we all liked to be, bright, cheerful, filled with things the children had made. Their arithmetic papers and stories were on the walls, terrariums filled with collections from our walks were on the shelves. A new mural was constantly being created on one of the walls.

Right now a huge orange pumpkin made from hundreds of pieces of crepe paper grinned down at us. Dan and I had only started it, the children had done the rest. We had thumbtacked large black background sheets to the wall. Dan had outlined the pumpkin and a few cornstalks in chalk, I had torn and pasted a half-dozen pieces of paper within the outline and then the kids had taken over. For the rest of the week they had worked on the pumpkin immediately after lunch while we sat finishing our coffee.

The old principle of imitation was at work here. All Dan and I had to do was start the pumpkin. When the kids saw me tearing up crepe paper (and I did tear more than I needed in order to tempt them) and pasting it within the outlines, they wanted to try, to do it too. No need to insist or to teach—only to let them take over and imitate—then discard the imitation and do it in their own way.

As I had learned from watching Helga, as Chris

and Brad had learned to eat and pee, so now our children were learning to live and work together.

In pairs or threes, they would set up assembly lines, Brian tearing up scraps of paper, Stuart smearing on paste, Tony fastening it to the wall. Other days, they worked separately, quietly.

There was a good feeling in the room, "good vibes," Dan said, and the worst punishment we could inflict was to banish someone to the hall for five minutes.

Little of the support we gave each other as teachers was planned, but over and over we built on each other's ideas and bailed each other out when we got in trouble.

The children could watch us, could see it working. Our children, all of whom had trouble relating to people, no longer had to watch silently as a teacher struggled to establish rapport with a child. Instead, here were two people who worked together all day long—people who kidded each other, withstood each other's mistakes without anger, who worked together and were more rather than less because of it. The atmosphere was contagious and the children began to kid us, to laugh, and to work contentedly alone and with each other.

Chapter SEVENTEEN

I had good news for Dan and I could hardly wait to tell him.

Finally he comes to school, looking bleary-eyed. "Sorry," he says, "I really had a bad night. Could hardly make it out of the sack this morning."

He hangs up his coat—the mornings are chilly now in late October—and takes his electric razor out of his pocket.

"Wait a minute," I say, knowing the second he turns on the razor the kids will leave their early-morning games and books and gather round him. They love to watch him shave—but I want to tell him the news and I can't in front of them.

"Listen, Dan. Guess what? They've okayed us at the Y. We can start next week."

"You're kidding! I was sure they'd stall you through the year." Even in a hung-over state Dan is satisfactory in his responses and I settle in to tell him, unable to contain my excitement.

"No, they didn't stall. I've got the official letter. I went over to see Mrs. Grady again yesterday after school, and she finally agreed and I waited while her secretary typed up the letter."

"Have you shown it to Doris yet? What did she say?"

"She said 'Fine.' We just have to contact the parents and get permission slips and have them send in suits and towels. Beginning next week, we can have the pool to ourselves every Wednesday from eleven-thirty to twelve. I did have to promise Grady that there would be only eight children, so that means only our class, to start; but I'm sure later we can work the rest of the school in ... also, we have to have at least four adults, so we'll have to line up two other people."

"Fantastic! That's great."

We had started planning this swimming program the year before. Dan loved taking the kids out of the school, and as we discussed possible trips swimming had come up. The idea excited me. It would put the children in a new milieu; it would let them see that they could function in an unfamiliar environment. It would provide a natural way of touching the children, communicating. It would teach them a new skill, make the long, hot summers bearable if they could learn to swim a little.

I had volunteered to get in touch with the Y. When I had been placement chairman for the League I had been there several times, arranging for volunteers to work in various programs. I had met Mrs. Grady then, and knew that she was community-minded; I felt sure she would open the pool to us if it was at all possible.

There had been difficulties. They had never had emotionally disturbed children there—the Board at the Y was concerned about accidents, lawsuits. Also, timing was difficult. Children were supposed to come in the afternoon, after school was out. Mornings were reserved for women's swims, elementary and advanced, and for the synchronized swimming group; noon hours, from twelve to two, were for the men. But our children went home at two-thirty.

Finally we found a day, Wednesday, when there was a half hour we could have: eleven-thirty to twelve. The time hadn't been booked because there had been no lifeguard available. I called Jane Farrow, an old friend from the League. I had seen her swim at the club, heard her mention having taken a lifesaving course. She said sure she'd do it; her bridge club started at one o'clock, but she was free all morning. At last all the pieces got put together and now, now, we could start.

At opening exercises that morning we discussed swimming in general. Nobody but Tony had ever been in a pool or a lake. Brian had seen swimming on TV, though.

"Gonna go to the ocean?" he asked. Brian was an avid television addict and he'd seen all kinds of rivers and oceans on television.

Alice's eyes lightened with interest and I could see her visualizing the exposed bodies, accessible breasts.

"What are we going to wear?" she asked.

"Bathing suits," I said. "Your mothers will get you bathing suits."

"The hell they will," said Stuart.

He had a point, we decided, and had a parents' meeting to explain the program. The idea met with little enthusiasm, especially from the mothers. They were sure that none of their children could learn to swim; they worried about colds, infection. Finally they agreed to let us try it for a month: we would report back. We then took the children on a dry run to see the pool from the glassed-in observation gallery.

That first Wednesday the children came to school carrying paper bags filled with towels and suits.

Jenny's driver carried in her paper bag, shaking her head. "Craziest thing I ever heard of," she said; "the kid can't even walk right and you want to take her swimming."

We had plenty of help, at least. Ourselves, Jane, the lifeguard, and Jerry, our psychiatric social worker. Later we would have a volunteer aide, but this first morning no one else had brought a suit. Jerry would help Dan. There would be six boys in the dressing room: Dan could use all the help he could get. I had only the two girls.

We separated in the large marbled entrance hall of the Y—men's locker rooms were down; ladies', up.

It was a long climb. I had told Jane she could go straight to the pool, that we could manage without her in the dressing room; so the two girls and I climbed the stairs alone. Halfway up I began to think that had been a mistake. Jenny wanted to go up on all fours, and I held her hand to keep her upright as she climbed slowly, slowly, one step at a time. Alice seethed with impatience, stamping her feet in exasperation.

At the top of the stairs was a closed door with a plump, gray-haired lady sitting at a table beside it.

"See your passes, please," she says without looking up.

I have no pass. No one had mentioned anything about a pass. "We're scheduled for eleven-thirty," I say.

"What? OHHH! These are *those* children. Oh, poor things. And you, dear. What wonderful work. What patience you must have."

I want to say, "I have little patience, particularly with someone as insensitive as you," but I can see Alice gathering saliva in her cheeks, preparing for a mighty spit, and I say only, "I'm Mary—this is Alice and Jenny. Is it all right if we go on in to get changed?"

"Oh yes. Yes. Of course, dear. Here are the keys for your lockers. The ladies' swim class has just finished, but there were only about a dozen women today. There are plenty of lockers and they should be through soon anyway."

Inside, there are rows of tall metal lockers with benches between, and cubicles for dressing with white duck curtains that can be drawn closed.

"Okay, Alice," I say. "We need to find lockers thirty-one, thirty-two, and thirty-three."

Just then a hefty redheaded woman appears from the showers wrapped in a scanty towel.

"Water's great," she says. "You girls here to swim with your Mom?"

Alice's eyes are fastened on the great mounds bulging over the top of the towel. "Mmmm-mmm. Strawberry," she murmurs in ecstasy. "Mmmm."

Alice still clung to her fantasy of ice cream breasts. She could draw well and in times of stress she would rush to the blackboard that covered the wall across the front of our room and begin drawing ice cream cones, waffle cones with large round scoops of ice cream, labeling each one with a different flavor. The chalk made hard, angry marks against the board as she wrote *vanilla breast ... strawberry breast ... butter-almond breast* inside each separate mound.

And now Alice gazes in fascination at the huge breasts protruding above the towel.

The woman, of course, knows nothing of Alice, and only says, "What, dear? What did you say? Well, have a good swim."

But Alice cannot let such delights disappear so easily, and with her eyes bulging she grabs the curtain before I can stop her, and flings it aside—disclosing the fat woman, sans towel, bent over, one foot through her pink underdrawers.

"Here now," she yells. "Close that curtain." And to me she says, "You ought to teach your children some manners—trouble with the world today."

"I'm sorry," I say.

"Alice," I say, "the curtain belongs to whoever's in the dressing room. She's the only one who can open and close it. Here, see, this will be your room; this is your curtain. Okay?"

Alice comes and moves the curtain back and forth. Forget the lockers for now, I think. The main thing is to get them in their suits before the whole swimming period is used up.

"Good," I say out loud. "That's yours. Your curtain. You do what you want with it—leave the others alone. Hang your coat up there, on that hook. Okay? Good. Now take off the rest of your clothes and put on your suit. Jenny and I will be right here in this one."

Alice is trembling with excitement, but she closes the curtain halfway and peers around at me. "Don't go away," she says.

"I'm right here," I say.

I open Jenny's paper bag and take out her suit, a navy blue puckered material. I lay it on the bench in our cubicle.

"Come on, Jen. Let's get our suits on." But she just hunches further over. I help her off with her coat. "You take off your sweater, Jen." She holds it to her. "Nnn."

I desert my goal of having her undress herself. Even if I achieved it, it would take the whole half hour of swimming. So I quickly peel the clothes from her slumping body; perhaps there will be more motivation for her to dress than undress. God, she is so tiny. She seems so fragile in my hands. I pull on her suit. "There," I say. "You're all set."

But the minute I let go of her she's out of the cubicle and running through the rows of green lockers, and I hear the fat woman say, "See that kid. Her sister's even worse. The mother has no control—can't handle them at all."

But all I am thinking is, She's running. Not bent over, but up straight; moving quickly, gracefully. And I smile at the fat lady as I catch Jen unexpectedly and lead her back to our cubicle, saying to Alice as we pass, "How're you doing, Alice?"

There is no answer, but I hear the pounding of feet, which means trouble, and I poke my head around her curtain.

Alice is naked, jumping up and down and at the same time trying to pull what must have been a size-three pink bathing suit up over her twelve-year-old body. I can feel the anger rise in me. What was her mother thinking to send that bathing suit? She can't deliberately mean to frustrate her. Is it possible she still thinks of her as a three-year-old child—or would like to?

Alice's mother had come to class one day, too shy to attend the regular mothers' meeting; she lingered in our class, telling me Alice was better—how grateful she was. But conversation was difficult, and I could not help but notice the long scars, some still unhealed, on her face and neck, and I could envision Alice, tall, strong, flying at this delicate woman.

Alice had attacked me several times. In the beginning I was unprepared and she caught me around the neck in a viselike grip, cursing, spitting. I pried myself loose and held her from behind, but she was strong and wrenched herself free and attacked again. I knew Dan was watching from across the room, although he gave no indication. He quietly included my other children with his own and continued teaching while Alice and I struggled.

I said nothing to Alice, too busy physically to talk, but as we held each other, forearms locked together, standing face to face, I said, "You don't hurt other people, Alice. It's okay to be angry, but say it in words."

She unlocked her right hand then and, forming it in a claw, she reached to rake it across my face.

I grabbed her hand and held her hard again and then she screamed at me, "But I can't do it. Don't you see? I can't do that problem!" Then she burst into tears. And I was more shaken by her words than anything else.

She couldn't do the arithmetic problem on the page.

"Oh, Alice, Alice lovey," was all I could think to say as I held her.

I was more careful after that. Alice was by far the most academically advanced child in the school. She had been in a private school for three years but they had refused to take her back, so her parents had enrolled her in public school in the suburbs where they lived. Two days later she was brought home after she had broken a chair across a desk, and she was put on home instruction until the waiting list at our school eased enough for her to be brought in. I learned now how little frustration she could tolerate, and I would go over each page with her first so I could be with her when she came to one she didn't know.

I also learned her noises. She would work quietly at her desk, but if she began to rock the chair back and forth—front legs, back legs—trouble was brewing. It meant that in minutes she would explode, and more valuable time would be wasted.

However, I did not believe Alice should be allowed to rule our classroom. I interrupted the pattern of violence as often as I could when I saw it begin to build. I would go and remove the paper or workbook and say, "Okay, Alice. Enough."

She was always surprised to see me, her own private world, so intense, so isolated, she hardly saw us most of the time—and as the volcano built inside her she saw us not at all.

"Alice," I would yell, because if I did not yell I could not penetrate; she would not hear me. "Alice, go draw."

Alice would get up then and the breasts would begin to fill the board, chalk breaking as she drew them in her fury.

Again, I longed for psychiatric help or training. I spoke to the staff, asking if they could see her privately; but there wasn't time. She was only one child out of twenty-four; she would need deep therapy. Even if they spent all their time with her, it still wouldn't be enough. She needed to be seen outside school, they said. I got the name of a woman psychiatrist with a reputation for excellence and called her; but she had no open time at present, so I gave her name to Alice's mother and was filled with frustration now myself. Who does have time? What kind of world is this when we don't have time to care?

I pondered Alice's drawing of breasts and took home her picture captioned FAMILY. It consisted of four faceless people: mother, father and small boy standing side by side on the right half of the paper. In the left corner, far away from the rest, there was an older girl, faceless as well, completely alone.

I asked Jerry, our psychiatric social worker, if he could make a house visit. Later he reported back that the Udalls lived in an attractive upper-middle-class development, but knew no one there. Mrs. Udall was a former violist—now she seldom left the house. Mr. Udall was an international banker, traveling most of the time from one European country to another.

The one time I met Mr. Udall he told me that he thought our school was excellent but that the curriculum needed strengthening. He stressed over and over that Alice should be getting more social studies—that we were quite weak in that area. Social studies! My heart wept and my head raged. Alice's mother shut herself in the house; her father escaped through traveling, avoiding, ignoring what she was. Alice needed so much more than social studies.

Jerry had recommended psychiatric treatment for the whole family, including Ira, Alice's brother, who was six years old now and mute. But as far as I knew nothing more had been done.

"Alice, wait," I say. I know she can never get that bathing suit on. "Wait just a minute." My own suit would be too big for her. I go back to the gray-haired lady at the desk, and she helps me find a suit in the Lost and Found that looks as though it might fit, and I think how nice people are underneath.

Alice loves the suit. A two-piece yellow, much like my own. She stands quietly as I fasten the shoulder straps and then pin her long blond braids on top of her head. Smiling, touching the suit, she says softly, "It fits me. Doesn't it fit, Mary? I'm big and it fits me."

Now there's only my own suit to get on. I am by now covered with a light perspiration, but at least the women swimmers all seem to have left. I go to the booth and start to undress but Jenny is up and away again, and so I go and bring her back and sit her down on the bench. Alice sits quietly beside her, and I simply stand in the doorway blocking Jenny's exit while getting into my suit. Alice appraises each part of my anatomy and says, "You're like me. Except you've got bigger breasts and more hair. But look, our suits are just alike. Two pieces."

"Right," I say. "We're lucky."

We hang our clothes in the lockers and go through the shower room, down the stairs, to the pool.

The boys are there before us, sitting on one of the long benches. Jane is in the lifeguard's chair. Jerry and Dan are sitting with the boys as we walk toward them.

"What a perfectly darling body you have, Mary," calls Stuart.

I can feel blood rise in my cheeks and an old shyness returns, but I know Stuart by now and I smile and say, "You look pretty good yourself, Stuart."

"Christ," Dan says, "I'm exhausted. How'd it go for you?"

"The same. What are we going to do now? Nobody seems very anxious to swim."

We decide to demonstrate. Since so much of our teaching is based on imitation, we think that if we swim and enjoy it visibly, perhaps some of the children will be moved to enter the water. Dan does three laps and then races Jerry, who turns out to be an excellent swimmer. Jerry's long mustache flashes from side to side as he churns down the pool and finishes ahead of Dan.

"Not as old as you thought, eh?"

Dan says, "You're good. I've got to get back in shape." And it's true that Dan seems to be smoking more than before.

I swim no races. But I do a lazy crawl and backstroke and blow bubbles and call and wave to the children. They sit, unmoving, on the bench, holding their towels, huddling together.

Only Tony comes close to the edge; finally sits and puts his feet in the water as I say, "Come on in, Tony. It's great. Really. Come join me. Here at the shallow end." Thinking if I can just get one started maybe the others will follow, I stretch my hand out to him.

But just at that minute a male lifeguard appears and shrills on his whistle. "Clear the pool!" he sings out. "Clear the pool for the Swim to Trim Program."

Half a dozen men of various shapes and ages appear at the far end of the pool, ordinary-looking men in conventional bathing suits. The lifeguard glows among them like a paste jewel, shimmering in tight white elastic nylon trunks, his chest bronze, his muscles bulging and quivering as he stretches his excellent body so that we can admire it better.

Once more he blows the whistle and flexes his arms above his head—and even before Alice reaches him I know what is about to happen. But I can't get out of the pool quickly enough to reach her; I can only call to Dan. By the time he comprehends what is happening, Alice is standing in front of the lifeguard, standing quietly in the soft yellow bathing suit, gazing at him in wonder. The guard is delighted with this attention and smiles, flexing his pectoral muscles now.

Alice says clearly, sweetly, "May I press your breasts?" Her palms rounding in anticipation, she reaches toward him, repeating, "Please, may I press them?"

The lifeguard stands speechless, his face horror-stricken, his arms folded protectively across his chest. Dan puts an arm around Alice and leads her away, "Come on, bear. Time to get dressed." And to the stunned lifeguard he says, "See you next week, Mac."

Upstairs, the three of us, Jenny and Alice and I, stand in our suits under the shower and let the warm water run over our heads and down our faces. Jenny stands beside me, and as she lifts her hands to wipe the water from her eyes I can see her fingers open and relaxed. A normal hand, no longer cramped and turned inward. Alice hums beside me, singing a little now and then. "My suit is like yours,

Mary. I'm going to be like you, have hair and breasts like you. We're lucky. Right?"

There is a close, warm intimacy there in the shower. I unbraid Alice's hair and let the clean warm water run through it. We know each other, we like each other, which is good because when we get out I make them put on their own clothes. This is hard, especially for Jenny, her hands moving slowly, awkwardly, but finally she is done and I hug her, and she stands straight again while I brush her auburn curls dry in front of the mirror. Alice's hair shines and I brush it too, until it hangs straight, free of braids.

Dan and the boys are already in the bus waiting for us. We are all very tired and very hungry and we know displeasure awaits us at school. We are over an hour late for lunch.

"What do you think?" Dan asks. "Was it worth it?"

Images fill my head—Jenny standing straight, running, unfolding her hands, dressing herself; Alice humming in the shower, saying, "We're lucky. Right?"

"Yes," I answer, "yes. For you?" knowing as much or more has happened with him.

"Yeah. Really good!"

And yet if anyone asked us we would have to admit that not one of the children had even been in the water.

I was gradually learning as a teacher why teachers' colleges were wrong to spend so much time on planning. The most important thing to learn was to be able to throw the plan away, whatever it was. What was necessary was to listen, to follow each minute to its peak, learning as you went. And this is difficult. It takes experience and self-confidence and courage. I had been lucky; Helga had these in abundance.

But what of the teachers in training now, learning to keep such careful records, to prepare to the final details, spending hours preparing materials to turn in for a grade from a professor?

If you have spent much time and energy in preparation, it is natural to want to cling to your plan, preserve all you have prepared. If I were ever to teach a college class, I would teach that a lesson plan should never be more than five lines long. A teacher should know where she is going, what her goals are, but a five-line plan can be easily discarded or postponed.

Instead of so much training in plan preparation, we should have training in reaction, role play with the unexpected. I would not advocate only spontaneity or tolerate laziness: I would also insist on tremendous amounts of background reading in learning theories, psychology, all fields of education. The goal would be to have the information so absorbed and internalized that what was most pertinent could be used at the right time.

Although our swimming program had gotten off to what might euphemistically be called a slow start, we continued. This, too, I was learning: to continue. Not to abandon a plan simply because it did not work well the first time or on a particular day. I was learning so much, so fast that it was hard to keep up with myself. That is, some parts of me were ahead of other parts, and I was excited all the time.

In any event, we continued with our swimming program at the Y, and gradually, gradually, it began to work. Some of the children stood on the steps of the pool, going a little farther each week until finally they were walking back and forth across the shallow end. The others we simply picked up and carried into the water, and they howled above our heads as we walked back and forth with them in our arms. Finally when everyone could stand alone in the pool we began games. At first, childish games—Ring-Around-the-Rosy, so that heads could duck under the water when we "all fall down."

"Jesus," Dan said, "if any of my buddies could see me now," as he and I and Jenny and Brian walked round a circle in the water.

Later we graduated to water polo and leaped wildly after the rubber ball; the children in their excitement would forget for a second or two that they could not, would not, ever remove their feet from solid contact with the bottom of the pool.

Rufus, surprisingly, was the first to allow me to put my hands under his white, pudgy stomach and guide him across the pool. Where he gathered his faith from I don't know, but he would say, "Help me, but go slow. Slower, Mary. Okay? Slow."

And we would proceed at a snail's pace across the pool with Rufus's head arched as far away from the water as he could get it, his eyes squeezed shut and his ordinarily pale face crimson from holding his breath.

We were strict about the deep end. No running along the pool edge or you were benched. The fact that this was a deprivation was progress in itself. No going to the deep end until you passed the Lifeguard's Test. I printed the rules in black ink on white oaktag and posted them in our classroom.

To pass the test you had to first swim back and forth across the shallow end four times; you had to float on your back; you had to be able to stay underwater for a count of twelve; and finally you had to swim the length with Dan or Jerry beside you.

Several of the kids were making it across the shallow end now, but it was Rufus who did the whole four widths first. In spite of his fears, he was the one who sought me out; he was the one who insisted we try again.

I discovered his motivation when I met his father at parents' conference. An intense, insistent, likable man, content with nothing less than perfection in himself and in others, he drove himself ten to twelve hours a day at the lab and then came home and worked on the old house they had bought till well past midnight, knocking down walls, opening up fireplaces. Carl Greenberg and his wife were young and bright and ambitious—and they viewed Rufus with a mixture of love and despair.

We argued, Carl Greenberg and I, about Rufus—something I rarely did with parents. I respected him too much to treat him with kid gloves.

"Rufus has to go to Hebrew School," he shouts at me. "He will go after he gets home from your school—but he has to go. How else can he have his bar mitzvah?"

"No," I say. "Not yet. Maybe never. He won't be able to do it now. It's much too difficult. He is only now learning our own alphabet, just beginning to read. If you make him, he'll fail, you'll get angry, and we'll be right back where we started."

"Oh! What do you know? Do you have a Jewish son—one boy—one eldest child? Do you know what it's like for him not to be able to do anything?"

I did not have a Jewish son, but I did know, could feel, the pride and concern and interfering I felt for my own son.

"Not able to do anything?" I ask softly. "Or not able to do what's important to you?"

For a moment I think he'll strike me, and then suddenly he leans back in the chair and sighs.

"Okay. All right, teacher, you win. What do you want me to do?"

"Just give him a little time," I say.

"Time!" He's shouting again. "Who's got so much time?"

And I cannot help but smile as I realize how much Carl Greenberg and I have in common.

With the desire for his son's bar mitzvah stymied, Carl Greenberg turned his energies to building a swimming pool, a large, plastic-lined pool set deep in the excavation he was digging in his backyard. It was to be ready by spring. Rufus dug with him on weekends; on Wednesdays, Rufus kicked back and forth across the pool.

The following April, Rufus asked if he could try to swim the length. There was nothing to say but yes.

He started off at the shallow end, Jerry swimming beside him, Jane, our lifeguard, poised on the edge, the rest walking along the side of the pool as Rufus kicked his way slowly toward the end.

It wasn't until they reached the middle that I realized I probably should have started him from the other end so that he could put his feet down if he tired or panicked near the finish. This way there was nothing to do but go on.

Five feet from the end, Rufus opened his eyes and raised his head to see where he was. In doing this he lost his momentum and his feet began to sink. Jerry moved closer, but I motioned him away. Rufus gasped and choked once or twice on the water he swallowed. . . .

I get down flat on the edge of the pool; lying against the cement, I stretch my arm toward him. "I'll give you a hand up, Ruf," I say.

His eyes focus and he begins automatically to kick, to move toward me—not only toward me but past me, past my outstretched hand, until he touches the edge himself.

The other children cheer and Rufus rests his head

against the end of the pool, then begins to feel his way down to the corner where the steps are. Slowly he climbs out, shivering, vision blurred without his glasses and I put a towel around his shoulders.

"I did it," he says. Then pulling the towel a little tighter around him, he looks at me fuzzily. "I did do it, didn't I, Mary?"

"Yeah, Ruf," I say. "You sure did do it."

We were even later getting back for lunch than usual that day; even Zoe was mad at having to keep food warm for so long. But it couldn't be helped: we had to stop and buy ice cream and cake to celebrate our first swim party.

Chapter EIGHTEEN

The swimming program was good, but Friday trips were better. Every child needs to get out of the classroom and explore the world, but for our children it was vital. Many of them knew only their own homes and the school. They had never been in a park, a museum or even a grocery store. They had never ridden a bus, a subway, a train, a merry-go-round or a pony. We did all these things on Fridays.

Here again, team teaching made it possible. It was a lonely, even dangerous thing for one teacher to take disturbed children in a car or in a crowded place. Explosion was never far away. But now both Dan and I found that all the children knew each of us well enough so that one could handle seven while the other took care of an emergency.

On one of the bulletin boards in the classroom we kept an ever-evolving list of trip possibilities. Whenever any of us had a suggestion we added it to the list.

On Mondays we voted on where to go on Friday. Everyone had his favorite. Brian and I loved picnics at the boat basin. We could explore the white yachts moored on the long piers; we could watch the fishermen pull in their catch; we could climb narrow, winding paths and finally eat at one of the picnic tables off the path. Sometimes we brought sandwiches; sometimes Dan cooked hamburgers on one of the grills.

Because we were a private school and because the Director also believed in our trips, and most of all because the parents were tremendously enthusiastic, there was little red tape. Things were kept simple. Each child brought in a quarter a week; when we had enough money for a train ride or bowling, they were included on the list. When there wasn't any money, we went to the nature center or the museum or the boat basin or the airport.

There was little formal planning. Whatever we needed we bought together.

No group of kids was ever better. There was no crying, no whining on long trips. The Volkswagen had become a second home to them and often they dozed as we drove back.

In November we had enough money to ride the train. We drove down to the station in the Volkswagen and parked it in the lot. The inside of the station was dusty, smelly, exciting—especially exciting buying a round-trip ticket to New York City.

We boarded together, Jenny's short legs barely making the big step; but then we separated, ranging out over the car, each choosing his own green upholstered seat, pressing his face against the window.

The children held their own tickets for the conductor to punch, waiting their turn with excitement. I knew that on Monday their stories, both oral and written, would be full of the train, the whistle, the noise of the wheels, the roar as we entered the darkness of the tunnel.

When we were well under way, Jenny moved over to sit with Alice, and Dan came and sat beside me, stretching his long legs under the seat in front.

"Can I talk to you a minute, Mary?"

I turned to look at him. He rarely called me by name, using instead the half-mocking, affectionate "Junior." He was still rumpled, rangy, attractive in a strong, loose kind of way. I felt a great wave of warmth and affection for him. Dan was good for all of us—he took the fear out of every situation: none of us were scared when he was there. We knew he would take care of us; he also believed we could take care of ourselves and we knew that as well. The result was confidence, and there is no more nourishing climate than this.

"Anytime," I say.

But Dan doesn't smile. Instead he says abruptly, "I'm going to fly down to Florida over Christmas."

"Florida?"

"I've been wanting to talk to you about this. There's a school there for emotionally disturbed children run by a man named Burmeister. I haven't met him yet, but we've been corresponding for several years. He had a great article in one of the journals a couple of years ago about emotionally disturbed adolescents, kids too old to stay in the few e.d. schools there are. Most schools are like our school, with a top age limit of twelve.

"There's no place for these teen-age kids to go if they haven't made it back to a public school yet. They're usually too young and too bright for a sheltered workshop and their families can't seem to handle them on a full-time basis; so they end up in institutions. And unless the family is wealthy or can borrow the money, the kid is put into a state institution and never comes out."

I shiver in the seat beside Dan and turn away from him for a minute, trying to erase the specter of an institution. The one in our state is huge and bleak and monstrous. Dan and I had visited it together one day, and we had come back more determined than ever to work harder with the children, be more patient with the parents, to find or create some other alternative.

Dan's voice is insistent beside me. "This guy Burmeister has gotten a school going that is part day school, part residential. He's gotten financial support from the state so that the cost to the parents is nominal.

"I'm thinking about next year, and the year after that. The reason I'm going down over vacation is that Burmeister is sounding me out about taking over his shares. I wanted to talk to you about it. What do you think?"

I look at Dan—the square, serious face, laugh lines already outlining the blue eyes at twenty-seven. He is a fine teacher, sensitive, committed, strong. He had taught science for three years in a secondary school before moving into special education, and he knows what his goals are for our kids. He should have a school of his own, a place to explore and build his own dream, not have to simply follow and execute someone else's.

Out loud I say, "It sounds right for you, Dan. You've always liked the older kids. They hold no threat for you."

"Would you come with me, Mary? We could finish the year here and then begin down there next fall."

My hand moves to cover his on the green upholstered seat. Only the outer part of me is surprised. Inside me, I think I have always known that we would want to keep teaching together and that the time would come when Dan would have to make his move away from Doris. "Thank you. But my own kids are in school here. I think this is where I belong."

The conductor calls our station and Dan stands up and the boys immediately surround him in the aisle. "Well," he says, "next year is a long way away. Just keep it in mind and I'll let you know more after I get back."

We walk all over Grand Central Station and then go out on the streets of New York. Cold, dirty, gritty—freaky people; a drunk with a tin cup pushes against me. A prostitute in a short red skirt and white boots approaches Dan with "Wanna go to my place?" and Dan grins at her as he leads us down the street. "Not particularly," he says. "I got my own place."

I love the city. I don't care how it looks—frumpy Broadway or elegant Park Avenue, they're all okay with me. It's the feel I like, the energy, the excitement.

But it's too much for the children. They crowd against us, overcome by the hordes of people, the volume of noise, the height of the buildings.

"How do people stay alive up there?" Rufus worries out loud.

So we ride the elevator in an office building to the twenty-seventh floor and realize suddenly that if some people look freaky to us, it's the reverse for other people.

A man in the elevator taps Dan on the shoulder to point out to him that Ivan, beautiful Ivan, has stepped out of his shoes so that he can whirl, turn faster, in the corner of the elevator.

"Put your shoes on, Ivan," Dan says and Ivan slows and slips his feet back into his shoes.

Again the man taps Dan's shoulder. "He's got them on the wrong feet," the man whispers.

"That's the way he likes them," Dan whispers back.

When we get off at the twenty-seventh floor, silent stares follow us out the elevator door.

The children plaster themselves against the window at the end of the hall, fascinated by the tiny cars and people below.

"How come they're so little and we're so big?" Rufus wants to know.

Dan laughs and puts an arm around him. "That's called point of view," he says.

Chapter NINETEEN

We spent the whole staff meeting discussing Brian's eating—or lack of it. We have kept careful records in school of what he has eaten and drunk, and his mother and father have done the same at home. The pattern has not changed: still he eats and drinks nothing but crackers and milk, and now he is almost nine.

There is improvement in communication, though. Brian is talking fluently both in school and at home, although he still uses more proper names than personal pronouns. But what delights me most is that his parents seem to be getting along better, talking to each other more, as well as to Brian and to us. Here is proof that a day school can work, that a residential setting is not always necessary. As the child grows, the parents, often for the first time, feel some hope, feel that someone is on their side trying to help with the ponderous burden they have been carrying alone. They continue to make mistakes, but so do we all. As long as we live we will make mistakes. The secret I'm finding out is to be able to forgive ourselves and one another.

By the end of staff meeting it was decided that Brian must eat. He could not develop normally without food. His parents would be asked to cooperate in not offering him food between meals; they would augment his diet of saltines and milk with vitamins and continue to keep a careful record of the food he ate.

We, Dan and I, would insist that Brian eat.

Dr. Marino had visited our classroom, a more lengthy visit than usual, and felt that our rapport with Brian and his relationship with us was strong enough now to withstand the pressure of being made to eat.

Staff meetings were held on Wednesday afternoons. Thursday morning before the children arrived, Dan said, "What do you think? Shall we start today with Brian?"

"Okay, fine. Let's go over it again."

We were going to ask that Brian eat one bite of lunch. Only that. Not a whole lunch—not a whole plate. Only a bite. His glass of milk would be poured like everyone else's (he was now drinking regular milk but he still refused the food). Now he would have to eat one bite of ordinary food, whatever was being served that day.

I think now we should have waited—at least until we knew what we were having for lunch that day. Or waited for a day when there was soup or even a noodle casserole, something that would have been soft in Brian's mouth—not so different in texture from milk and soggy saltines. But then, too, we did not realize we would have frankfurters on rolls that day. It was a first.

The morning had been a good one. The kids had worked on their arithmetic and each read in his own reading book, and we were writing a story about swimming at the pool at the Y during language arts.

At lunchtime Tony set the table, his turn that week. Stuart poured the milk. Ivan put around the napkins while Tom sat on a high stool watching and reciting the Gettysburg Address.

Brian was at the blackboard, starting to draw the telethon for cerebral palsy that he had watched the night before. I went and stood beside him. How to tell him? How to prepare him? I tried to think of the right way, but it would not come and time was running out. I would tell him as best I could.

"Bri," I said, "you're doing a good job. You've learned to talk and read and hike; yesterday you got in the water at the pool. Today you're going to learn to eat."

"Crackers? Gonna eat good crackers?"

"No. No more crackers. Today you're going to eat food. Like me. Like Dan. Okay?"

Brian began to flutter and hop up and down.

"No food. Brian doesn't want food."

"One bite today, Bri. You take one bite of food today."

"No food. Only crackers. Brian will eat some nice saltines—from the little baker."

Dan came over and said, "Forget the little baker, Bri. Here comes Zoe with the lunch. Today we eat, buddy."

Tears welled in Brian's eyes, but he followed me to the table and sat down.

Dan lifted the lid from the covered heating cart and said, "Kee-rist."

"Don't swear out loud in here," said Stuart.

"What is it?" I asked.

"Nothing," said Dan. "I mean—it is something. Something new. A treat. Yep, a real treat. Hot dogs on rolls. Just like at the ball game."

He rolled his eyes at me and held one up.

Never had a hot dog looked so long, so red—so unconsumable. Beside me, Brian said, "Gonna go home now, Mary. Brian's gonna go home."

"Brian and I will share a hot dog," I say to Dan. "Here, put it on my plate." I knew he couldn't stand

seeing that huge roll and frankfurter on his plate:
even if he didn't have to eat it all, just the sight of it
would make him panic more.

I cut the hot dog into two pieces—two thirds for
me, one third for Brian—and put it on his plate.

"Gonna go home now. All through. School's all
through now, right?"

"We're going to eat now, Bri. See. Watch me." I
spread mustard on my roll and then put one end in
my mouth and bit through the roll and hot dog.

Brian watches closely.

"Oh. Oh," he says, "poor Mary. Good-bye, Mary.
See you tomorrow."

He gets up and starts to leave the table. I take his
hand and pull him back down again.

"Your turn now. Do it just like I did. Put it in
your mouth and bite."

Brian closes his mouth and presses his lips together—his face turns red and he shakes his head
from side to side, "Nnnnnn-Nnn," he says through
his clenched teeth.

My own voice comes out harder now. "Yes, Bri.
One bite. Remember. You are going to eat one
bite."

"Nnnnn-NNNNN." He starts to slip under the table, reminiscent of days with Chris.

I put my arm beneath his armpit and pull him up,
keeping him close to me.

"Hey, now. Come on. You can do it. It's not that
hard, really. Look at me again."

I take another bite; the hot dog is cold by now.

"Okay. You try it."

He squirms away and I pick up his piece of roll
and hot dog and put it to his lips, still keeping one
arm around him.

He spits when the roll touches his lips and pushes
against me, and I say, "Listen now. You're going to

eat one bite today. We're going to stay here, you and I, until you do."

A threat? Maybe, but not an idle one—I am prepared to stay the rest of the afternoon.

Dan joins us. "What's all this? Hurry up. Eat your lunch, Brian."

Amazingly, Brian picks up the hot dog and lifts it to his mouth and I think, Ah, good—this will soon be over. But just at the second it reaches his mouth he turns and flings the frankfurter and roll across the room.

Dan picks it up and brings it back, jamming the hot dog into the roll, jamming the whole thing into Brian's hand.

"Forget that stuff, friend. You're going to eat it. Now get with it."

Tears are streaking down gentle Brian's face now. I feel like crying myself. Dan, huge, immovable, stands over Brian and myself.

Between tears and gasps Brian says, "Just the roll, okay? Brian will eat one bite of the roll. The nice soft roll. Right, Dan Franklin?"

Brian nibbles at the side of the roll like a small mouse, a few crumbs entering his lips. And I would have settled for that. That was far enough for Brian to have come in one day.

But instead I hear Dan's voice saying, "A hot dog on a roll has two parts, the roll and the hot dog. Okay, you ate the roll. Now one bite of the hot dog."

Oh, Dan, you ask too much. But I do not, cannot, desert you.

I cut off a small piece of my hot dog with the mustard knife and eat it slowly, chewing with my face close to Brian's, my arm still around him.

"Actually," I say, "it's easier this way. See, Bri. About five good chews and it's ready for swallowing."

Brian will have none of it. He throws the hot dog across the room again—Brian, who has never thrown anything.

"Goddamn it, you don't throw food in here. Now you get it and bring it back." Dan's voice fills the room.

Brian gets up, but instead of heading for the hot dog he runs toward the door.

Stuart says, "Don't swear in here, Dan," very self-righteous now that he has stopped swearing himself.

And I look and realize that all seven kids are watching us in fascination.

"Cool it, Stuart. Just cool it," Dan says as he takes Brian by the shoulder and leads him to the hot dog. Brian picks it up and we start again.

This time Dan sits in another small chair behind Brian and pushes a piece of hot dog into his mouth.

Brian spits it out.

Dan sticks it back in.

Brian spits it out.

"For Christ's sake, swallow it. Swallow the damn thing," says Dan.

Zoe comes in to clear away the dishes and pour us coffee.

"Oi-yoi-yoi-yoi-yoi," she says, raising her eyebrows. "I guess you won't be wanting coffee today."

I nod in agreement and she passes out Drake cupcakes to the rest of the class. "I'll be back to see if you need me," she says. And I nod to her gratefully.

Dan himself is now perspiring, great wet patches beneath his arms. He leans back in his chair, gathering strength, holding Brian against him. There is no anger in him now, only resolution. They could almost be lovers, there is so much tenderness in the way he holds the boy.

Then he says, "No joke, Bri. Today's the day that you're going to eat."

Brian shakes his head in negation and they begin again.

I cannot help but feel surprise—and some sort of admiration for the spirit inside this pale, pudgy boy that keeps him resisting. He is strong; he can do all sorts of things if that strength can just be channeled.

Dan crams the piece of hot dog in. Brian spits it out.

"Maybe some water would help," I say. A poor suggestion.

I put the hot dog in and Dan dumps water from a paper cup quickly into Brian's mouth.

Brian spits it all out. Now we are all wet with sweat and hot dog water.

Zoe opens the door. "Want me to take the kids to the park with the other classes?"

"Please," I say. Dan and Brian say nothing—just sit back resting as though between rounds.

When all the kids are gone, Dan says, as much to Brian as to me, "All right. How are we going to work this now?"

I have no ideas and just sit, facing Brian. Brian sits resolutely in his chair, and even when Dan gets up from behind him and walks to the window to light a cigarette, Brian doesn't move. He no longer runs for the door, no longer even cries—just sits with his mouth clamped shut until Dan returns.

"What we'll do," Dan says to me, "is get the hot dog in and then hold his mouth shut so he can't spit it out. I remember I got my dog to swallow a pill that way once."

"All right," I say. I am not convinced but I know without question that we are all committed now, Brian as much as us, and there is nothing to do but play it out.

"You put it in, Mary. I'll hold his mouth closed."

I force Brian's small white teeth open and put a

piece of hot dog the size of a thimble in his mouth. Quickly Dan closes his big hand under the boy's chin.

"Good. Okay, Bri. Now swallow. All right. Good. That's it."

Dan takes his right hand away. Splat. Out comes the hot dog on the floor.

"Get another piece, Mary. Put it in again. Farther back this time. Swallow it, Bri. Swallow the damn thing," Dan shouts in Brian's ear. Brian never says a word—just spits it out.

All afternoon this continued. All three of us were wet, exhausted.

When the kids came back from the park it was two-twenty. Zoe looked at us. "I don't believe it," she said, and took the rest of the children to wait in the office for their buses.

At two-forty-five she came to our room again. "Brian's driver is here," she said.

"Get his coat," Dan said to me. I brought the blue plaid jacket.

"Put it on him."

As I pushed his arms into the sleeves Dan kept pushing the hot dog back into his mouth. Then with one arm around Brian's shoulders and one hand over his mouth he led him to the taxi.

When Dan came back to our room I was still sitting at the scene of the battle. "Oh, Dan," I said, "that was so awful. I'm sure we did it all the wrong way."

Dan sat next to me, put his arms on the table, his head on his arms. "Yeah. I know. But what's the right way? Who knows a right way? At least we did something."

"Did he finally swallow it?" I asked.

"I don't know. All I know is that when I put him

in the taxi door he still had the damn hot dog in his mouth."

I got to school early the next day. So did Dan. I knew we were both wondering the same thing: Would Brian be back? Would his parents come in? How about the Director? Perhaps we had lost Brian for good.

At exactly nine-fifteen exactly the same as any other day, Brian appeared in the doorway and said, "Good morning. Gonna draw the men. Johnny Carson. Frankie Laine. Yule O'Toole and Perry Como. Saw them all on TV. On the telethon. Gonna draw it on the board now. Okay?"

And he hung his jacket on the hook beneath his name.

All morning I was edgy. I didn't see how we could stand a repeat of yesterday.

At eleven o'clock I excused myself and went down to the furnace room to find Zoe—to find out what we were having for lunch.

She looked up from the hot tray. "You won't believe it," she said.

"What?"

"Baked beans with sliced hot dogs."

"Oh, no-o-o."

I told Dan as we set the table.

"Jesus. Well, here we go again."

"Oh Dan? Are you sure . . . ?"

"Pour the milk, okay?"

Zoe wheeled in the cart and then waited in the doorway as I served the children. Lots for Tom, Dan, Ivan, and Tony—medium for Alice, Rufus, Jenny, and me. Just a spoonful for Brian.

I sat down and started eating without comment.

And next to me, out of the corner of my eye, I saw

Brian pick up his fork and carefully, carefully spear one baked bean and one slice of hot dog.

Don't say anything, I think. Eat your own lunch. Let him keep his dignity, his privacy. Let him do it his own way.

Quietly I see him raise the fork to his mouth—and I look around the table. There is no sound; everyone is eating his own lunch. Seven pairs of children's eyes watch Brian. Dan and I watch each other.

Then Brian pokes me. "Gotta eat one bite—right? Not just the bean. One bite of both. Look at it." He opens his mouth to show me the bean, the hot dog slice, so that there will be no mistake.

"Right," I say.

His face contorts. He chews—once, twice—then swallows and grabs his milk.

Dan raises his own paper cup of milk. "Here's to Bri," he says. "Let's drink to Brian, King of Hot Dog Palace."

Even now I think that what we did was wrong. There must have been some better way. When I think of Brian and the hot dog now, I think of it mainly as a lesson in how much children can survive, as an example of one of the many mistakes I made that should have hurt the children but somehow didn't. But perhaps Brian knew that he must eventually learn to eat in order to survive—and that it was our responsibility, as adults and teachers, to insist that he do so. Perhaps he recognized the loving that we felt.

Each day from that time on Brian ate a little more, balking at new foods sometimes but eating more and more—at home as well as in school. At a parent's conference his mother told me happily how he made his own sandwiches on weekends—ham on rye bread.

Many months later, we talked about this. I had been asked to speak at the state convention for psychologists, and as "a token of appreciation" they sent ten dollars to the school. The Director gave it to me, saying, "You earned it. Use it any way you want."

I took my class to Howard Johnson's with the money, just four of them and myself, and said, "Order anything you want. The sky's the limit."

Brian sat beside me, tall now, almost eleven, handsome in his blue plaid shirt. "Two franks on rolls and a side order of french fries," he told the waitress.

As we waited for our lunch to come, I said to Brian, "Do you remember the first time you ate a hot dog?"

He turned his fork on the white and orange mat in front of him. "Yeah," he said. "And Dan Franklin yelled in my ear, 'Swallow it. Swallow the damn thing.' "

I wished he would have told me more—told me why, how—but he couldn't. Nor did I ask for more. There was enough absolution, enough happiness, for both of us in his order of two franks with french fries on the side.

Chapter *TWENTY*

Transitions are important—in school as well as in grammar. A child can fall apart as easily as a paragraph, with meaning and content lost, if the transitions are not well carried out.

I was concerned about an upcoming transition for Stuart. He had made such fantastic progress since that first day (A, B, C, D, E, Fuck). From no reading at all, he had moved through primers, first grade, second grade—and now was reading on a third-grade level. This, of course, was far below grade level for him; he was almost twelve now. Still, it was a long way to come in a year. I was particularly concerned about Stuart's move because of his age. The other children who had left had gone into elementary schools where classes were small and the pace at least relatively slow. But if Stuart was to make it in a public school, it would be a junior high. The junior high in his town was housed in an old brick building, overcrowded now but still maintaining its good academic rating. I had gone there alone a week before to talk to the principal, who had then referred me to the head of special services. They did have a class for e.d. students and I asked if we could visit.

There were twelve students, working on various levels, with the teacher, male, about thirty, moving from desk to desk. I talked to the teacher about the class, about Stuart. Both of us were hopeful. It seemed as though it might work.

"Why not bring him in next week? It's a short week—just the three days before Thanksgiving. We're not going to get an awful lot done anyway," the teacher said.

When I asked Stuart, however, he said flatly, "I'm not going."

"Why not?" I asked. "It's just to look."

"Yeah? Well, I don't want to look. I'm gonna stay in this crazy baby school."

A typical Stuart remark—need phrased as insult.

Still, he had grown. He was a pleasure now on trips, capable, helping with the younger ones. He worked eagerly on his academics and was getting along better with the other boys, although his sharp tongue still made them regard him with caution.

Volunteers had a difficult time in our room because of Stuart. He effectively excluded them because he wished to be taught by us, not volunteers—and as Dan had told me those many months ago, Stuart had an uncanny knack for getting to a person.

The first volunteer who came to our room was a Junior Leaguer, young and tall with long blond hair. She was intelligent, finely bred, courteous. As she leaned over Stuart on her second morning he smiled up at her, eyes blue and deceptively innocent behind his thick steel-rimmed glasses, and said quietly, "What do you usually use for your halitosis?"

She got herself assigned to another room.

Even our psychologist, Dr. Steinmetz—a rotund man with curly gray hair and a full beard—seldom came to our room. He had tested Stuart, and Stuart desired no more testing. When Dr. Steinmetz appeared in the doorway Stuart would carefully inquire after Weight Watchers, feigning surprise when Dr. Steinmetz said he knew nothing about it.

In the beginning, Stuart had tried to get rid of me, too. On one of our Friday trips we rode the

Staten Island ferry, and before we were halfway across the bay he had cleared our side of the ferryboat of all but a peaceful drunk and me.

Every time someone sat down next to him on our bench he began to swear in a soft, clear voice. "Fuck. Shit, Son of a bitch. Bastard." If his language didn't drive them away, he farted, raising himself on one buttock, almost seeming to take aim, then saying, "Oh, excuse me. I seem to be having trouble farting."

I didn't leave. I didn't even say anything, although later I would tell Stuart and enforce it that if he wished to swear he was to do it under his breath; he did not have the right to disturb other people. But I couldn't really think of anything appropriate to say. Inside me, I knew what was happening. Stuart was saying to me, "I'm testing you. Nobody loves me. Nobody can love me. I'm too awful. I trust no one. Not you. Not anyone. You'll leave me too. See, you can't take this. You'll go soon, like all the others." This was no time for discipline; that would come later. This was a time for loving. So I sat in my navy blue double-breasted coat looking out the window at the brown waters of the Hudson while Stuart aimed his ass at me and neither of us spoke.

Back at school, our relationship grew, but slowly. Stuart would stand by the door flicking the light switch on and off, on and off, gazing unblinkingly at the ceiling light fixture. His fascination with light bulbs and switches was paramount—on and off, on and off—sometimes I thought he longed to control us the way he could the light switch. In any event, any fact, word, or number that Stuart had difficulty remembering I could teach him easily by drawing a light bulb around it in colored chalk—and "comprehend" or "7 x 12" was fixed forever in his head.

He used touch in an odd way. If he had had a difficult morning, immediately after lunch he would begin to fiddle with the light switch, then he would revert to his old trick of kissing Dan's hand—finally he evolved one for me. He would deliberately wet his forefinger and then as I bent to sip my coffee, he would move quietly behind me and slip the wet finger into my ear.

And he'd get his response. Startled reaction would snap my head up, coffee spilling on the table and me, and Stuart would smile, finally satisfied, and go to play his collection of favorite records.

We held each other once, though without tricks or games.

During reading I had put a relatively easy compound word on the board, asking the children to divide it, spell the separate parts, use the whole word in a sentence. I always put new words on the board before the children encountered them in their books, and I always asked the child to use the new word in a sentence in which the context of the sentence defined the meaning of the word. This way I knew that he understood it, was familiar with it—and the word was now his to use as he wished.

I did this while the word was on the blackboard because I wanted books themselves to retain the feeling of success, not to be the place where a child had to struggle with a word. This way when a child met the word on the printed page he already knew it and said, to himself at least, "This is an easy book."

I write COBWEB.

"C-o-b—cob. W-e-b—web," says Tony.

"Good, Tony. Use it in a sentence, Stuart."

"Uh. Cobweb. There were cobwebs in the cellar."

Unexpectedly, Stuart puts his head down on the table.

"Okay," I say, "but tell me more. Lots of things can be in a cellar."

But Stuart doesn't raise his head.

"Stu, are you okay?"

No answer.

I leave the blackboard and go to his desk, and he raises his head just long enough to take off his thick eyeglasses and cram a handkerchief against his eyes.

I squat beside the chair. "In the cellar?"

"Yeah, yeah, the cellar. That day. There were cobwebs all over the bottles in the corner. The kind with metal squirters on the top."

Stuart raises his head. "You know? You know the kind I mean?"

I nod.

"I liked to squirt 'em but I knew I wasn't supposed to be down there. My mother didn't like me down there when I was little. She said it was dirty. All of a sudden I heard somebody coming down the stairs and I hid. It was Daddy. He took big, slow steps and I hid in the corner where he couldn't see me.

"He sat down on the washtubs and took a bottle out of a bag and drank, sort of moaning.

"I got scareder, but I didn't know how to get out of there without him seeing me. I wasn't supposed to know about the bottle. When they thought I was asleep, my mother would yell at him to leave it alone. Anyway, after a while he got up and I was glad because my legs hurt so much from sitting on them, but he didn't go away. He just went over to an old army trunk, got it unlocked, took an old gun out, and then he stood there—and after a long while he shot the gun in his head."

I don't speak, though my insides ache for him; I know I have to let him finish, without touching him, without interrupting.

Stuart slams his hand against the desk and then again harder against my shoulder.

"In the head. In his fucking, shitty head. Then he fell down. I was too scared to come out. I thought he'd get me if he knew I'd seen him. So I stayed in the fucking corner and wet my pants. I couldn't help it. A long time later my mother came down and turned on the lights, and yelled—and I ran—and—and . . ."

The sobs began then, building until they drowned his words and he reached for me. I half pulled him out from behind his desk and held him. We walked to the wall and leaned against it, still holding each other. Then when he had quieted, I got my coat and his and signaled to Dan; and we went outside and walked around the building and then across the street through the cemetery, neither of us saying anything.

The main thing I wanted Stuart to know was that I wasn't going to leave him. I was there, no matter what.

I called the psychiatrist at lunchtime to find out what I should do—how to handle it, thinking perhaps he should come in, talk to Stuart himself. "No need for that. What you did was right. That was fine." And I thought, There must be more.

Now I realize what a unique position we were in. Where a child psychiatrist could see a child once, twice, three times a week for an hour at a time in a specialized setting, we saw our children five hours a day, five days a week. We learned with them, we played with them, we ate with them. We lacked psychiatric knowledge, but we had a deep and special knowledge of the child. I knew none of this then; felt only that Stuart had trusted me with a secret part of him, had given me some sort of key to himself, and I wanted guidance so I would use it correctly. I talked to the Director, asked if I should call

Stuart's mother. She said yes, that I definitely should. I called, and Rita Wagner came in the next afternoon. She was tall, in her early thirties, with the statuesque body of a showgirl and long black hair.

I told her as gently as I could what Stuart had told me.

"Who'd believe it?" she said. "He was only four. I didn't think he even remembered. Charlie drank a lot. Always did. But then he lost his job and I went back to working as a waitress—more a hostess, actually. Charlie's drinking got worse, and then he got this crazy idea that he had cancer and that we were all hiding it from him. We couldn't talk him out of it. Not the doctor, not me—nobody. So he drank more and more so he wouldn't have to think about it. Then one day he just went down in the cellar and blew his brains out. And Stuart's right—I found him down there hiding in the corner and carried him up the stairs and got my next-door neighbor to take him to her house. But I didn't think he remembered; he never mentioned it. Look, let me show you."

She opened her pocketbook, her wallet, and took out a faded picture of a small redheaded boy. "See? That's what he looked like then. He was such a beautiful little kid. The fellow down the street even wanted to put him in a movie, he was so beautiful. Everybody said so." She sighed and put the picture back. "Of course, that was before he got so crazy-acting."

The important thing was, she loved him. I knew she did. She wouldn't carry that picture around, or come in right away when I called her, taking off from work, if she didn't.

Everything was going to be all right. She loved him. Stuart was going to make it.

I thanked her for coming in, for talking to me; and showed her Stuart's reading workbook and spelling papers. All she said was, "Who'd believe it? Who'd ever believe it?" I was not quite sure what she was referring to, but it didn't matter. I knew she was going to be on his side and I knew the odds were good that he was going to be all right.

The thing was, though, I had made it pretty clear that I wasn't going to leave Stuart. He could count on me. I would be there. But the fact remained that he was almost twelve, and by the rules of the school this was his last year.

I pondered solutions. It seemed that the thing to try to do was to get him to want to leave school himself. Finally he agreed to go and look at the junior high, extracting promises from me—written at his insistence in red Markalot—that I would not leave him there. So on the day before Thanksgiving vacation Stuart and I left Dan and the other children and drove to the junior high in my car.

We arrived as classes were changing, and the contrast between our own small sunny room and the huge, dim corridors of clanging lockers and halls jammed with superstar kids could not have been more pronounced.

I thought Stuart might be frightened, but his ability to insulate, isolate, himself stood him in good stead, and while he seemed to have pulled on a plastic covering he also seemed interested.

We proceeded on down to what would be his classroom. Officially it was called a "traveling class"; this meant that the kids in the class were gradually integrated into the regular classrooms, at first staying in the homeroom most of the time; then gradually, as their abilities and emotional stability increased, they "traveled" to more and more regular classes. Some moved totally out of the traveling class and into a regular classroom at the end of a year. Others stayed there throughout junior high. Either way was all right with me: both were a long way from the institution.

Stuart feigned his bored, superior air when I introduced him to the teacher, but he looked good; I was proud of his cool.

Back in the hall on the way out, Stuart pointed to the green lockers and addressed me:

"Would I have one of those?"

"Yes. Sure. Everybody has one. That's where you keep your coats, books, things like that."

"Do you get a key? I mean, you know, your own key? So you can open and close it when you want to?"

"Sure," I said. Then another thought occurred. "Listen, Stu, do you want to see the cafeteria?"

"What do you mean?"

"Come on," I said. I should have thought of it earlier. Food was far more interesting to Stuart than a classroom.

We went down and walked through the cafeteria. Stuart was filled with awe.

"You mean they have three kinds of soup on the same day? You're kidding? Three kinds, and you get to choose what you want?"

Obviously Stuart had become a convert. No more need for a sales job here. I was suddenly conscious of the hour, of the fact that we were late for our own lunch back at school.

I nudged Stuart along, though he was in no hurry now, lost instead in admiration of the fluorescent lights that lined the ceiling. All those and three soups too. We would hear about this the rest of his remaining time with us. Happiness and hunger mixed inside me.

"How'd it go, Stu?" Dan asked as we came in.

"Okay. Where's lunch?"

"Right here. We decided to wait for you and Mary

so we could hear about the school. Go wash and we'll get it set up."

Zoe had served the other classes and then left the hot cart in our room. While Stuart went to wash I decided to get the lunch ready—I'd skip washing today. It was late; I'd save time.

I went over to the hot cart, intending to push it to our waiting lunch table. It seemed to be slightly stuck. I pulled harder and it came loose—not only came loose, but shot out from the wall, wavered back and forth, and then fell sidewise, crashing against the tile floor.

Zoe had put the coffee pot on the bottom of the cart and plugged it in to keep it warm, and I had not looked closely enough to notice. When I pulled, the plug resisted, then came loose, and the sudden jolt tipped the cart over.

A gigantic pool spread at my feet, brown liquid coffee mixing in the dumped-over casserole of franks and beans. I looked at it in horror: they'd waited for us and now I'd ruined everyone's lunch. It was unsavable; coffee grounds floated on top of the beans.

Tony came over to my side and surveyed the mess with awe. "Gee, they look just like black ants crawling on the beans, don't they?" he volunteered.

Dan said, "Get the pail, Tony. Ivan, you get the mop."

Dan himself got the garbage can.

There were no recriminations, no accusations. We all mopped and scraped; even Jenny unfurled her cramped fingers and helped me wipe the last sticky residue from the floor.

"I'm so sorry."

"Couldn't matter less. Glad to get rid of those beans. Right, kids? Right, Tom?"

"Right, Tom," Tom said.

When the floor was clean I went down to the fur-

nace room and told Zoe, who helped me find the
peanut butter and bread she kept in a corner of the
refrigerator for emergencies. I carried them back to
our classroom, and the kids and Dan and I sat
around the table while I spread cold peanut butter
on unbuttered bread, making sandwiches for all of
us.

We ate them with delight. Once again, disaster
had not torn us apart; only made us closer. They for-
gave me my mistake, as I suppose I had theirs, and
there was a feeling in our room that day that we
could do anything.

The kids laughed and ate their peanut butter
sandwiches without complaint. As for me, it was the
nicest lunch I'd ever had. I knew it was corny; I
knew it was sentimental. I also knew it was something more. And I valued the more.

Unexpectedly, Dan tilted his head back and
laughed out loud.

"What's funny?"

"We are. Me particularly. Didn't get married—
wanted to play the field, keep my freedom—right?
And now look what's happened right here in school.
We've turned into a goddamn family."

And he was right. That was the more. We were a
family.

Chapter *TWENTY-ONE*

I had forgotten how beautiful my own children are. It has been a long time from September to Thanksgiving, and I can hardly take my eyes off them when I first see them. I drive to Elizabeth's school, pick her up, meet her roommate, her teachers, and then we drive back together, talking all the way. Rick arrives that same night, Wednesday, in his battered car, and we all hug each other and laugh. We have never been apart from each other for this long before, and it is important to catch up on everything that's happened—Rick's courses, soccer, the new girl he's met; Elizabeth's roommate, the lesbian science teacher, the election that made her secretary of her class. We don't mention the divorce at all; we had been over it thoroughly earlier, and there was, I think, a desire inside all of us to make our brief holiday together as happy as possible.

All the time they talk I memorize them. Elizabeth's slim body now turns with grace; her neck arches like a young colt as she tosses her long black hair back from her forehead; and intensity lights her face as she leans toward Rick to say, "But wait, listen to this. We were supposed to . . ." and the rest of her words are lost to me as I etch the entirety of her being into my mind.

Rick has not changed as much; only grown more what he was. His handsome, regular features seem somehow larger, his brown hair longer, curling at the base of his neck. Gone is the little-boy look. He lights a cigarette and leans back against the couch, relaxed, talking easily, one boot resting on the opposite knee.

I lean forward and talk now, too, telling them about the children at school, about the various theories of childhood schizophrenia, talking about causes, environment, the biochemical makeup of the child.

"Is it the parents, Mom, do you think? If they had loved their child more, would he have been all right?" Elizabeth asks.

"I don't think it's that simple—love. I think too often educators, researchers, doctors, take that as an easy way out. I don't care for Bettelheim's huge stone mother built in the courtyard of his treatment center so that the children can kick her, let out their aggressions—although I do agree with other things he says. But this seems too easy to me, almost like saying to the parents, 'You have almost destroyed this child. Now we'll try to help, try to undo the damage, but who knows how much we can do now?' Saying this absolves therapists or educators of responsibility—if there's improvement they can say, 'Ah, see what we have done.' If the child remains the same or regresses they can say, 'Ah well, too much damage had already been done.'

"It seems to me more complex than that; these same parents often raise other normal children. I think there must be a combination of causes. I'm sure the parents are important, but there must be something else, something inside the child himself, specific to him, maybe a different body chemistry, maybe a tremendous sensitivity that means he's hurt more easily than other children by factors in his environment. But the thing that strikes me most is the uniqueness, the enormous individuality, of each child, despite the superficially common symptoms.

There is no one picture, no one description, of a schizophrenic or autistic child."

We talk again in the morning, through breakfast and extra cups of coffee, through stuffing the turkey and putting it in the oven to roast, through our late-afternoon Thanksgiving dinner.

Too soon it is Saturday afternoon, and the children go to visit Larry and attend the holiday dance at the club. After they leave I clean up their debris with reluctance; the apartment is lonely without it and I stay for a long time on the little porch, looking after Rick's car that is no longer there. Finally I shiver in the cold and go back inside.

With the children gone for the day and night, I begin to read, an old solution to loneliness. But I find I cannot stay lonely long. I am so excited by the thoughts inside my head.

I am still taking courses in special education, gradually accumulating the credits I need for certification; but these education courses don't seem to be answering the questions I am seeking answers to. How do we teach most effectively? How do we educate? What is education?

I go back and reread parts of Erikson, and then start on Fromm and Rollo May—and come back to teaching and involvement.

The teacher, any teacher, must be involved—involved with the subject that he's teaching, with the children he's teaching, and preferably, demandingly, with both. What is school anyway but a preparation for the rest of your life?

Okay. Then how do you get these teachers, the ones who are willing to be involved? Where do you find them?

I don't know. Don't know. But I know that I will be one. And when I have learned how, I will continue to learn more, and all the time I will welcome into the classroom any new teacher who wishes to learn whatever I know.

It is a disgrace to the teaching profession that it is so difficult to "place" student teachers, that colleges pay out a paltry bribe of sixty dollars or so to a teacher who will take a student teacher. Ah, Helga, I wish you were here so that I could argue with you. You would tell me that the children are the important thing. But I would tell you what I have now found out. You are unique, but you will not live forever; you must allow others to learn from you.

All right. This is nothing new—practical teacher training, in-classroom training, is being touted all over now. What "new" is there to that? Okay. One new thought is to offer these master teachers credits rather than money if they must be offered something. In our degree-mad society, let them earn credits, instead of dollars, for their work training young teachers, because without fail the older teachers will learn from the younger ones as well.

My head pauses, but not for long. Back to involvement: what is it? What do I mean? I mean a very active force, energy going back and forth between two or more people, an excitement, a caring. A caring? A loving? Do I dare to say loving? Could the community, could the schools, could the parents admit, dare to admit, that there should be loving in our schools?

No matter what they admit, this is what I think. Not only should there be loving, there must be loving, in our schools. Tough, strong, responsible loving by people who can accept other people's weaknesses and ignorance—and their own as well. They must accept and then attempt and act, taking the responsibility for the consequences the actions bring. Because there is no real loving without action and responsibility.

The loving to which I refer must be better than

what we ordinarily mean by loving. As the laser is beyond light, this, too, must be more.

The laser fascinates me; I review the acronym, made up of letters from the words Light Amplification by Stimulated Emission of Radiation, and consider again how the laser consists of ordinary light, but light that has been concentrated, channeled, directed, so that it is fine, true, delicate, powerful.

Ah, the words form in my head. That is what I will have. Laser teaching: Love Amplified by Structured Educational Reality. This is what we need in our schools. This is what I must learn to practice. But as the laser must be handled with knowledge and skill so that its power does not damage, so my laser teaching would require intelligent, sensitive teachers.

An idealistic dream? Perhaps, but I write it in big letters on the kitchen blackboard, happy, happy, with the thought. Then inside my mind I write it once again before I go to sleep.

Chapter *TWENTY-TWO*

Jenny Woodriff came back from Thanksgiving vacation wearing bright red corduroy overalls exactly the same color as the wagon in the back of our room, and this became her favorite spot. Each day after lunch, while Dan and I drank our coffee, Jenny perched in the wagon surveying us like a small gnome.

I had known Jenny first at the old school. She had been in Nick's class, and occasionally his class had joined Helga's for walks to the village. Helga knew, as Dan did, how important it is to make the children a part of the world and the world accessible to them.

One day Nick had asked me to keep track of Jenny on our walk. You could not hold her hand, curled tight as a bird's claw. She walked doubled over—thin as a matchstick, long, skinny arms swinging back and forth, hands almost touching the ground. I tried simply to keep in body contact with her, my thigh against her shoulder, my hand occasionally pushing back the heavy wool bonnet that she continually pulled down over her eyes.

Unexpectedly a truck had roared by, close to us, loud, noisy, and Jenny had turned and screamed. Screamed and wound her arms around my legs, burying her face against me, then turning, pointing, still screaming words or almost words as she pointed to the truck that thundered by.

Nick had come then and taken Jenny, and I had

moved to walk beside another child—but what remained indelibly in my mind was Jenny's response. Though it was terror, she had responded. Though she turned her hands inward and her body downward, she had not yet turned herself off. She still responded. And if this was true, she could be reached—and that meant she could and did still learn, and that we could teach.

But the next year, in Renée's room, I was not so sure. She was one of the children who lay on the floor in the cold, wet bath water. In fact, she began to go deliberately—or so it seemed to me—to the puddle of water around the tin tub to move her bowels. This was when Renée had explained to me that Jenny thought she was a dog, that it was part of her hate, her revolt, and that she must be allowed to express it. It was also when I had gone to the Director and asked to be transferred to another room.

Renée did not return the following year. Jenny was assigned to our room, and Dan loved her from the first instant, claiming her for his class. Whatever toilet-training problems she had had before had been resolved over the summer, and though her cramped body posture continued and she pulled her curly hair down over her eyes and nose, leaving only her mouth visible, nonetheless I would catch brief glimpses of a smile as Dan sang to her at beginning exercises, "A frog he did a-courtin' go, mmhmmmmhmm," or carried her high on his shoulders as we jogged around the duck pond.

I knew Jenny best at the swimming pool. Here Alice, Jenny, and I struggled each week with the problems of showers, dressing and undressing, haircombing, and coping with the ladies from the synchronized swim class. Fearful at first, gradually Jenny learned to love the water, and as the weeks went by she began to paddle back and forth across the shallow end of the pool, her hands, her whole body, relaxed and mobile.

What puzzled us most, however, was her lack of speech. Her gentle mother would come to conferences each week and ask the same question each time: "Did Jenny say anything yet?" And always we had to answer, "Not yet," sometimes adding, "She climbed on the bike of her own accord," or "She set the table for us this week"; but never had we heard a sound from Jenny. In our class there had not even been the scream of two years before.

She did talk at home. Not to her brothers or sisters or her father; but she spoke to her mother. Each week Mrs. Woodriff would tell us of their talks. Jenny whispered, spoke so that only her mother heard, but spoke in full, complete sentences.

In school she not only didn't speak—she didn't make a sound. Not a cough or a hiccup; even her footsteps were silent on the tile floor. Silently she sat in the wagon; silently she surveyed us.

But if Jenny loved the red wagon, Brian loved Jenny. Of all the children in the school Brian loved Jenny the most. Whenever possible he tried to sit beside her in the bus, read his book out loud to her, give her his cupcake at lunch. But Jenny acknowledged him not at all, wrapping her coat around her, pulling her hat over her eyes, pretending she never saw the cupcake Brian offered.

Now, though, as she sits in the wagon she is more vulnerable, more accessible, and Dan and I watch as Brian gently invades Jenny's isolate world as we once invaded his.

It has taken him a week or more, but he has gotten Jenny to let him sit on the table beside the red wagon and hold the long handle as he talks to her. He tells her the details of each telethon and joke after joke. "What happened to the cat that drank the lemonade, Jenny Woodriff?"

Not a glance from Jenny.

"He turned into a sour puss," and Brian laughs so hard he has to get off the table. Although Jenny tries she cannot keep her smile totally inside.

Three days later, Jenny lets Brian pull her around the classroom in the wagon. He walks backward, slowly, slowly, talking to her the whole time, and Jenny unfolds her hands and grips the sides of the wagon—but she stays in and lets Brian pull her.

And now, now, he pulls her in the hall. We go to collect the mail in the office, Brian, Jenny, and myself—Brian pulling Jenny down the hall at a rapid clip.

There is a large carton for us. Books. More books, and I am as excited as the children. We get the carton into the wagon and Brian hops up and down with excitement. "Sit on the box, Jenny. Sit up high on the box in the wagon."

And Jenny does. Now back down the hall, Jenny teetering in the wagon, excited by the ride, the prospect of the package. Brian goes still faster, I trot to keep up—and suddenly Jenny laughs out loud. Not a small laugh, a large, loud, huge laugh. And Brian stops dead and stares.

Then he drops the handle and covers his ears. I take my cue from Brian and cover my ears too.

Jenny looks at us in delight and laughs even louder. She is in control now. There it is, as clear as a bell. Jenny is making us do something rather than the other way around. And she loves it. What to do? How to make this work?

Ahhh. I keep my own hands over my ears and say to Brian, "It's a good thing Jenny doesn't laugh much. Too much noise."

Brian? Does he know? Will he help?

He nods his own head, ears still covered. "Too much noise. Right, Mary. She makes too much noise."

Jenny, of course, laughs even louder all the way back to the classroom.

Alice doesn't like the noise at all and goes to the board to draw her ice cream breasts, vanilla-ha, chocolate-ha, jumping up and down as she draws; but at least she doesn't spit or throw the chair.

Stuart watches Jenny benignly, hand inside his pants. "What a baby girl," he says. "She could really mess up in here if she knew how to swear instead of just laugh."

"SHIT!" shouts Jenny. "GODDAMN SHIT!"

And I could almost hug Stuart. But Dan and I merely unpack the carton and study the new books. The kids are doing the teaching now. Stuart has helped Jenny move from a noise to words; what words they are does not matter just now. I hope that she will move to other words in time; I hope also that Stuart will one day no longer put his hand inside his pants. But even if he does, that is not what's important. These children of ours will always have their problems; very few make it all the way back. What is important is for them to make it to the public school so that they are able to live with their families.

Jenny swore for two days—loud enough to bring the Director down the hall from her office. Jenny yelled swear words from the moment she arrived in the morning, through flag salute, through academics, through lunch, art, basketball, and swimming.

We were all sick of it, Alice's breasts covered the walls now as Dan taped up the ones she painted on the newsprint paper. Yellow, blue, and black laughing breasts. We were all sick of it except Stuart. He followed Jenny, teaching her new words, whispering to her, while Jenny shouted, "FUCK! BULLSHIT! CRAP!" and the Director said merely, "I hope the nuns don't come today."

I waited. Boredom would come soon. Swearing is not that interesting by itself.

By the third day there was a lag, and I merely followed Stuart's lead by saying, "I don't mind the swearing or the laughing—I can tune those out—but God help us if Jenny ever reads out loud."

I knew it was obvious. So did Jenny. But the thing was, it let her save face.

She looked at me. She looked at Dan. Then she took her reading book from her own cubbyhole and screamed at us the title of her book: "A HEN IN A FOX'S DEN."

She went to her red wagon, folded her legs tailor-fashion beneath her and screamed the first lines of the first page: "Rag was Jim's pet. Kit was Dot's pet cat."

Not until our Christmas party ten days later did she talk to us in a quiet voice. In fact, it wasn't even to us. Jenny spoke to Brian. Standing upright, handing him three cookies she had made as presents, she said softly, "Merry Christmas."

Brian's hands flapped against his sides. It was too much. The excitement was too much and he couldn't keep them still. But even so he took the cookies, let them flutter, too. "To you, too," he said, "Merry Christmas to you, too, Jenny Woodriff."

From then on Jenny spoke to all of us, not screaming now. There was no need—that had only been the key she used to open the door of speech for herself.

Chapter *TWENTY-THREE*

Christmas arrives and, though I know all the things that are wrong with it—commercialism, endless buying to make up for lack of love, pushing crowds and all the rest—still I love it and I am excited when we go to buy our tree.

We are going to have a party at school, and the biggest tree that we can find. Our room is a double room and it can hold a big, big tree. The other teachers already have their trees, small and neat on their windowsills, pretty and almost real, trimmed with tiny blinking lights and tinsel. But we will have none of this; we must have a huge green tree that reaches from floor to ceiling with strings of colored lights and paper chains and ropes of cranberries and popcorn.

We go together, the whole class, ten of us, to the parking lot behind the Y and survey the field of Christmas trees. We all go in different directions, calling to each other: "Look at this one ... How about this one? ... Oh Dan, look, this one is perfect."

Finally we narrow the choice to two, the tree man holding first one and then the other, stamping them in the snow, shaking them to loosen the branches to show how fresh they are. We debate, we examine them, comparing height and symmetry, and finally the agonizing choice is made. Ah, we have been right; it is obviously the best tree in the whole place.

The tree man offers to carry it to the car; but no, we must do it ourselves, each of us holding a tip, a branch, a piece of the trunk, marching down the driveway. Our tree. Suddenly Dan leaves the tree to us and sprints ahead, getting out his camera—always Dan has his camera in the black case across his shoulders, calling back to us to stop, to wait a minute while he snaps a picture.

We must have been a funny-looking group: tiny Jenny standing upright now, but hands still cramped and tight; sullen, golden-haired Alice; the six boys hopping up and down with excitement, with an occasional flap or twirl. The tree man watches Dan take the picture and then calls to him with wonder in his voice: "Hey, Mac, are they all yours? Boy, you and the missus sure must have your hands full."

"What? . . . all ours?" It takes Dan a minute to grasp the full meaning. "Oh—*ours*. Yeah. Sure, they sure are. They're all ours."

The children hear. They know. Our lonely, funny children who have never been part of anything, who have lived for so long behind the walls, the locked doors, of their homes. Now a stranger looks at them and thinks that they are part of a family and Dan does not deny it. His loveliest Christmas present to them.

"Did you hear what that guy said? How about that?" Dan exults, delighted, laughing, sprinting back to me, whispering, "He must think you're some sexy broad, having all those kids. Hmmm." Dan rolls his eyes in what is supposed to be an obscene leer.

"Everybody knows that," I whisper back. "Older women desire more." I roll my own eyes.

We stand laughing together, thinking we're funny, until I feel Jenny shiver and recognize the cold, and we trot the rest of the way to the VW and Dan ties our tree on top of the bus.

We make a mess in the classroom, pine needles all over. At least eight inches have to be cut off the tree; we overestimated, or maybe it's under. Anyway, there has to be room for our star at the top, and we all argue and push and crowd Dan, telling him how much till he gets impatient and shouts, "Give me room!" But finally it's up and Dan wires an extra branch in a place that doesn't seem to have one, and we all declare it beautiful.

The rest of the week we trimmed our tree. We popped popcorn on a hot plate and did our arithmetic counting out the snowy corn. We had white strings of popcorn and ruby-red streamers of cranberries—as much on the floor as on the tree but somehow it didn't matter. We made a wreath for our door out of pine branches and red velvet ribbon, and a centerpiece for our table from pine cones. Mornings were for academics. I was the taskmaster here, insisting that we continue with our reading, the number line, the tens and ones columns. We had come too far to let the learning slip.

Happiness filled the classroom, though we were all a little high from overwork and anticipation of the coming vacation. Dan was flying down to Florida to see Burmeister about the school for next year. I already had my ticket for Mexico and would leave three days after Christmas to complete the final formalities of the divorce on January second.

But for now there was Christmas, and we planned our party with care.

We didn't get much done the morning of the party; the great pile of wrapped packages under the tree was too much to ignore. Each of us squeezed and pinched and poked whenever we could, trying to discover secrets, until finally it was time and we sat in a circle around our huge, beautiful tree while Dan distributed the presents.

Brian, a red snap-on bow tie beneath his chin, sits beside Jenny Woodriff, talking softly to her. She has already given him the three Christmas cookies she made, and every once in a while she speaks to me now, too, in a normal voice. Leaning across Bri, she calls, "Merry Christmas, Mary," as if she likes the sound of the words.

Ivan sits quietly in his socks, whirling his shoes in front of him. His shoes whirl, but he controls the rest of himself, at least during the hour of our party.

Tom leaves his spot and goes to stand beside Dan.

"Okay, Tom. Help me deliver. Here, this one is for Stuart from you."

"For Stuart," says Tom, and then on his own, with his turtleneck turned down, he adds, "Merry Christmas, Stuart."

Stuart is fascinated by the tree, the lights, the glitter and shine, but he moves his eyes away from the tree and accepts the package from Tom. "Thanks, buddy," he says, his voice as much like Dan's as he can make it.

Alice sits close to me, her shoulder touching my own. I had tied red bands of ribbon in the girls' hair before the party and Alice touches hers now and says, "It's pretty, Mary, isn't it?"

"Yes," I say and hug her. "It's pretty and so are you."

And she was. (But Alice wasn't one of the ones who made it the next year. Though she was observed at our school in the spring and accepted for a public school program, I heard secondhand that she lasted only three days before she spat in the teacher's face and threw an eraser across the room. She was put back on home instruction. I felt then and I still feel sorrow and frustration for not having done a better job. All that teaching, all that growing, but she wasn't able to make a transfer. Yet a teacher of emotionally disturbed children must be able to accept failure and still feel that each minute step these children make is as valid as a leap for someone else. Perhaps somewhere, someone has managed to reach Alice.)

On the other side of me sits Rufus, wearing his best blue suit and a sober expression.

"What's the matter, Ruf?" I whisper.

"I'm Jewish," he says worriedly. "Jewish people don't believe in Christmas. Do you think it's all right for me to be here?"

"Of course it's all right. It's our party. It's for all of us. We'll have another one for Hanukkah. Okay?"

A smile breaks through. "You mean it? You won't forget? We'll celebrate Hanukkah?"

"Absolutely," I say. "We've got lots to celebrate."

And we did. We were all there, we had all survived: the hardest part, the first half of the year, was over, and our room was no longer bedlam. We were able to sit quietly around a Christmas tree, sharing. The children were all speaking and eating now—though to varying degrees—all beginning to learn to read and write and communicate with each other. Of course I knew, Dan and I both knew, that the children weren't *cured*—that they would always be different, more isolated or more violent; still there was hope that they would be able to live in their own homes, their own communities. Actually, it was not so much that they were different from other children; rather, in these children the anger, the loneliness, the frustration and the confusion that are part of all of us were magnified, amplified. Perhaps in this magnification, this amplification, we can find some of the causes of loneliness and anger; and if we can find the causes, perhaps we can find a few of the answers for all of us.

Across Rufus's head I smile at Dan.

We had stayed late the afternoon before, counting to make sure that the presents for the children would come out even, that no one would be disappointed. And they weren't. There was a surprise for each child from us, and from each other. Everything had to be made or cost less than a dollar. There were the usual orange-juice cans painted to look like pencil holders—looking instead like painted orange-juice cans—endless packs of cigarettes for Dan and bath powder for me; and for the children, balls, crayons, pictures, candy. Nothing was special; everything was.

At the end of the day, after the children had gone and we had cleaned the classroom, put it back in order for vacation, and donated our tree to the Sunday school, Dan and I sat in our classroom drinking a last cup of coffee.

I had given Dan a scarf for Christmas, put it under the tree with the other presents. I had found blue yarn and knitted a long blue scarf for him the same color as his eyes. He wore it now as we sat on the desks drinking coffee.

Suddenly he gets up and goes to the closet in the back of the room and takes a flat brown package from the top shelf and comes back and lays it across my knees.

"I gotta run, Junior; my plane leaves in a couple of hours. Well, anyway. Here. This is for you."

But he still stands in front of me, the blue wool scarf incongruous with his shirtsleeves but exactly the color of his eyes. Then he reaches out, one big hand cupping my face, turning it up to his.

"Merry Christmas, Mary. Take care this vacation. I'll see you in January."

He closes the door quietly and I stay on the desk with the flat package on my knees, listening to his Volkswagen turn over, then catch and drive away. I open the package carefully, lifting each piece of Scotch tape without tearing the paper.

Inside are lines from one of e. e. cummings's poems, scribbled in black ink on framed parchment paper.

> i carry your heart with me (i carry it in
> my heart) i am never without it (anywhere
> i go you go, my dear; and whatever is done
> by only me is your doing . . . .

I get up then and walk around the room, carrying the poem with me, touching the blackboard, the books, the chairs and tables, the coat hooks with our names labeled over them. I trace each letter of his name.

Cummings had said it for us. In our teaching we had become a part of each other. Wherever, whenever, I taught from now on, Dan would be a part of that teacher.

There is a strong urge, a compulsion almost, to define that teacher; the teacher I hoped to become.

I reach for paper, pencil, and write my title, "Teacher," across the page.

It was dark when I finished, and much of what I felt was still unsaid, but I tacked my poem to the bulletin board just inside the door to give to Dan his first day back.

Chapter *TWENTY-FOUR*

In Juarez, Mexico, the sadness of divorce proceedings belied the gaudy veneer of punchbowls and bright signs lettered WELCOME TO FREEDOM.

There was something frantic and false in the celebrating, and I headed for the shower each time I returned to my hotel room.

It was hard to imagine that one day I would be able to recall Larry with only a neutral kind of tenderness. Now the divorce brought back memories, and thinking of Larry was like touching a bruise, tender and aching at the edges, more so at the center of its blue-black heart. The hurt was less when I didn't touch it, but time and again my mind moved back to go over it, like a tongue on a sore tooth.

In any event, it was done. Last year's tax purposes were served and now I was eager to be done with Mexico and mourning.

Our plane circled New York before landing, and the city shone like a Christmas jewel that night, clear and bright and beautiful—full of promises for the New Year.

Chapter *TWENTY-FIVE*

I arrived at school the next morning breathless from the cold and the prospect of seeing Dan and the children. But Doris cornered me as I went through the office on the way to our room.

"Oh, good morning, Mary. Happy New Year. Did you have a good vacation? Looks like a cold day today, doesn't it? My. Well, as long as it doesn't snow. There's always enough trouble the first day back without bad weather as well. Oh, incidentally, I wanted to tell you: Dan's been detained."

"Detained? What do you mean, detained?"

"Well, an emergency. In Florida. Some man, Burmestman, or something like that, died. So Dan had to stay on for a while; said he'd tried to call you but there was no answer at your apartment; wanted me to give you the message."

"A while?" I say. "How long is that?"

"Well, actually, probably quite a while. A few weeks, months . . . well, one never knows, does one?"

Does one?

A skinny youth appears beside Doris; he impinges on the periphery of my vision. A new student: No, too old for that; and my thoughts go back to Dan. What could have happened? Burmeister died? Ah, that would be hard. Especially if it happened while Dan was there; if there was no one else to take over . . . I can understand that, but why . . . ?

"Mary? Excuse me, I don't think you heard me. I said this is Claude, the new teacher in your room."

I couldn't believe it. This skinny boy a teacher? Could Doris already have replaced Dan? Already hired someone to take his place?

I put out my hand and smile as best I can. It is not his fault; whatever has happened, it certainly is not his fault, and it must be difficult for him. Had the sinking of my heart shown in my face?

"Hello, Claude," I say. "I'm glad to meet you."

Claude blushes and smiles and nods, too filled with embarrassment to speak.

I follow Doris back to her desk. "Is Dan coming back? And if he is, why have you already hired someone to take his place?"

Doris smiles, skirting the issue in familiar style. "Oh, well, you never can tell what will happen. I had this feeling that Dan was getting a little too big for his britches—you know what I mean. It won't hurt him to know he's expendable. Claude's a good teacher; you can call him a substitute, if you like. I thought it would be a little hard for you to handle eight children alone, Mary."

Again, there is no one to blame. Dan in Florida when Burmeister died. ... There would have been pressure on him to take over—and he loves it there. And it will be good for him. He will have his chance, his opportunity, to build and run his own school. Right, Mary? And Doris—how can you blame her? Dan and she weren't getting along well. It must have been a relief to her that Dan has been "detained."

And Claude? Not his fault. He had only said yes when asked. Nothing to blame in that.

But oh, God, how can I teach without Dan?

How will I live through each day without Dan? What will I tell the children? How can this Claude handle Ivan and Tom and Tony and little Jenny?

I walk to the office window and press my head against the cold glass, trying to focus on the immediate day, on an approach to the problems ahead. I am not sure I have the strength. And I am tempted for a moment to walk out too. To put my coat and gloves back on and leave again—leave the problems to Doris, to Claude, the substitute.

Substitute. The word rings a familiar bell, and I remember the day when I first came as a substitute. It was just this time of year. Winter cold. Snow close behind the gray clouds. Everyone busy, involved, with no time to tell me about the children or show me what to do.

Can I now do this to Claude?

Suddenly I remember Helga—Dan—the Director, too—my teachers, and all that they taught me.

Now it's my turn.

I bend and tie the laces of my sneakers a little tighter and then walk over to where Claude stands self-consciously by the office door.

"All set?" I say. "Did you get some coffee? Okay then. Good. Let's go on down to our room and I'll tell you about the kids on the way."

Down the long, dim hall, through the door of our classroom, past the bulletin board, the coat hooks labeled with our names, MARY—DAN. Past the blackboard to the bookcases beneath the window.

"See," I say. "Here are our books. And the workbooks . . ."

I look away to steady my voice a little. I look out the window of our classroom and see Brian's bus arrive. He clambers out, his small, bright, pointed face pale and vulnerable in the morning light, his hands flapping gently against his sides.

He looks up and sees me at the window. The flapping slows and he raises his hand and waves—and then moves quickly, surely, to the door.

Teacher

I will know you.
I will touch you and hold you
And smell and taste and listen
To the noises that you make—and the words, if any.

I will know you.
Each atom of your small, lonely
Aching, raging, hurting being
Will be known to me
Before I try to teach you.
Before I try to teach
I must first reach you.

And then, when I have come to know you, intimately,
I will insist, gently, gradually, but insist
That you know me.
And later, that you trust me
And then yourself.

Now, knowing each other, we will begin to know the world—
The seasons, the trees, animals, food, the other children,
The printed word, books,
The knowledge of what has gone before and been recorded.

Then as surely as I moved toward you
I will move away.
As I once insisted on being close to you,
Demanding entrance to your half wild world
Of fear and fantasy, refusing you aloneness,

So now, I move away.
As your words come and your walk quickens,
As you laugh out loud
Or read clearly and with understanding,
I stand behind you—no longer close—
Available, but no longer vital to you.

And you—you grow!
You are! You will become!

And I, the teacher,
I turn, with pride in you,
Toward my next child.

Other SIGNET Books You'll Want to Read

- [ ] **YESTERDAY'S CHILD by Helene Brown.** A mother's searing story of her struggle to save her tragically handicapped daughter—and herself. (#J8500—$1.95)

- [ ] **LIKE THE LION'S TOOTH by Marjorie Kellogg.** A beautiful novel about children who somehow find within themselves the raw courage to lighten their dark world. "Not since Richard Hughes's *High Wind in Jamaica* has a novel about children so played upon my sympathies."—Edward Weeks, *Atlantic Monthly* (#Y5655—$1.25)

- [ ] **LISTEN TO THE SILENCE by David W. Elliott.** A total and unique experience—gripping, poignant, most often, shattering. A fourteen-year-old boy narrates the chronicle of events that lead him into, through, and out of an insane asylum. "Each page has the ring of unmistakable truth . . . a well written tour de force, another *Snake Pit* . . ."—*The New York Times Book Review* (#Y6588—$1.25)

- [ ] **36 CHILDREN by Herbert Kohl.** "An extraordinary and heartbreaking account . . . Mr. Kohl tells, with great simplicity and honesty, what it is like to be a teacher in a public school in Harlem."—*The New York Times* (#E8438—$1.75)

- [ ] **I NEVER PROMISED YOU A ROSE GARDEN by Joanne Greenberg.** A beautifully written novel of rare insight about a young girl's courageous fight to regain her sanity in a mental hospital. (#J8737—$1.95)

SIGNET Books of Special Interest

☐ **THE CHILDREN ARE DYING by Ned O'Gorman.** An unflinching portrait of the savage dehumanization of kids in Harlem —and a deeply moving personal record of a struggle to stop this modern massacre of the innocents.   (#E7960—$1.75)

☐ **WORDS FOR A DEAF DAUGHTER by Paul West.** Not since *A Child Called Noah* has there been such a poignant portrait of a child's private world. Mandy is isolated from the world by deafness and possible brain damage. This is the story of her discovery of the natural world and of how what might have been a tragedy grew into a joyful celebration of life.
(#E9091—$1.75)

☐ **AUTOBIOGRAPHY OF A SCHIZOPHRENIC GIRL with analytic interpretation by Marguerite Sechehaye.** The astonishing personal story of a flight into madness—and of the difficult path back.   (#Y7812—$1.25)

☐ **IF YOU COULD SEE WHAT I HEAR by Tom Sullivan and Derek Gill.** A blind man's triumphant, inspiring life story . . . "Get to know a remarkable young man who packs more into his life than most sighted people."—*Boston Globe* With an 8-page photo insert.   (#J9376—$1.95)

☐ **THIS STRANGER MY SON by Louise Wilson.** The harrowing, moving story of a deeply disturbed child—told by the mother who struggled for years to free him from the prison of mental illness. "Intensely moving . . . an extraordinary book written with simplicity and humility."—*Book World*
(#E8729—$1.75)

Buy them at your local

bookstore or use coupon

on next page for ordering.

SIGNET Books of Special Interest

☐ **ONE, TWO, THREE: The Story of Matt, a Feral Child by Eleanor Craig.** The unforgettable true story of rescuing an emotionally disturbed child against heartbreaking odds . . . "Remarkable . . . upbeat!"—*Boston Globe* (#E8841—$2.50)*

☐ **DAUGHTERS AND MOTHERS: MOTHERS AND DAUGHTERS by Signe Hammer.** Here is a book that can help you understand how the bond between mother and daughter can enable the daughter to become a strong, "free" woman or keep her tied to her mother in a mutually dependent relationship that allows neither of them to grow. (#E8721—$1.75)

☐ **I WANT TO KEEP MY BABY! by Joanna Lee.** Based on the emotion-packed CBS Television Special starring Mariel Hemingway, about a teenage girl in grown-up trouble. The most emotion-wrenching experience you will ever live through . . . "It will move you, touch you, give you something to think about."—*Seattle Times* (#W7649—$1.50)

☐ **MARY JANE HARPER CRIED LAST NIGHT by Joanna Lee and T. S. Cook.** Here is a deeply moving novel and sensational CBS TV movie that brings the full horror of child abuse home. A rich, spoiled, and emotionally disturbed young mother, abandoned by her husband, takes her frustrations out on her little girl . . . "Powerful, riveting, stinging, revealing!"—*Hollywood Reporter* (#W8045—$1.50)

* Price slightly higher in Canada
